D0595062

KADAMPA TEACHINGS

PREVIOUSLY PUBLISHED BY THE
Lama Yeshe Wisdom Archive

Becoming Your Own Therapist, by Lama Yeshe
Advice for Monks and Nuns, by Lama Yeshe and Lama Zopa Rinpoche
Virtue and Reality, by Lama Zopa Rinpoche
Make Your Mind an Ocean, by Lama Yeshe
Teachings from the Vajrasattva Retreat, by Lama Zopa Rinpoche
The Essence of Tibetan Buddhism, by Lama Yeshe
Daily Purification: A Short Vajrasattva Practice, by Lama Zopa Rinpoche
Making Life Meaningful, by Lama Zopa Rinpoche
Teachings from the Mani Retreat, by Lama Zopa Rinpoche
The Direct and Unmistaken Method, by Lama Zopa Rinpoche
The Yoga of Offering Food, by Lama Zopa Rinpoche
The Peaceful Stillness of the Silent Mind, by Lama Yeshe
Teachings from Tibet, by various great lamas
The Joy of Compassion, by Lama Zopa Rinpoche
The Kindness of Others, by Geshe Jampa Tegchok
Ego, Attachment and Liberation, by Lama Yeshe
How Things Exist, by Lama Zopa Rinpoche
Universal Love, by Lama Yeshe
The Heart of the Path, by Lama Zopa Rinpoche
Teachings from the Medicine Buddha Retreat, by Lama Zopa Rinpoche
Freedom Through Understanding, by Lama Yeshe and Lama Zopa Rinpoche

FOR INITIATES ONLY:
A Chat about Heruka, by Lama Zopa Rinpoche
A Chat about Yamantaka, by Lama Zopa Rinpoche

IN ASSOCIATION WITH TDL PUBLICATIONS, LOS ANGELES:
Mirror of Wisdom, by Geshe Tsultim Gyeltsen
Illuminating the Path to Enlightenment, by His Holiness the Dalai Lama

LAMA YESHE DVDS
The Three Principal Aspects of the Path • *Introduction to Tantra*
Offering Tsok to Heruka Vajrasattva • *Anxiety in the Nuclear Age*
Bringing Dharma to the West • *Lama Yeshe at Disneyland*

*May whoever sees, touches, reads, remembers, or talks or thinks about these books
never be reborn in unfortunate circumstances, receive only rebirths in situations
conducive to the perfect practice of Dharma, meet only perfectly qualified
spiritual guides, quickly develop bodhicitta and immediately
attain enlightenment for the sake of all sentient beings.*

• • • •
•

LAMA ZOPA RINPOCHE

Kadampa Teachings

Edited by Ailsa Cameron

LAMA YESHE WISDOM ARCHIVE • BOSTON
www.LamaYeshe.com

A non-profit charitable organization for the benefit of all
sentient beings and an affiliate of the Foundation for
the Preservation of the Mahayana Tradition
www.fpmt.org

First published 2010
15,000 copies for free distribution

LAMA YESHE WISDOM ARCHIVE
PO BOX 356
WESTON
MA 02493, USA

© Lama Thubten Zopa Rinpoche 2010

Please do not reproduce any part of this book by any means
whatsoever without our permission

Library of Congress Cataloging-in-Publication Data

Thubten Zopa, Rinpoche, 1945-
Kadampa teachings / Thubten Zopa, Rinpoche ; edited by
Ailsa Cameron. — 1st ed.
p. cm.
Includes bibliographical references.
Summary: "The Kadampa geshes were exemplary practitioners of Buddhism
in Tibet, renowned for their extreme asceticism and uncompromising prac-
tice of thought transformation in order to develop bodhicitta. In this book
Lama Zopa Rinpoche, himself an exemplar of these practices, explains the
Kadampa geshe approach, basing his teachings on 'The Bodhisattva's Jewel
Garland,' Lama Atisha's wonderful text on developing bodhicitta"
—Provided by publisher.
ISBN 978-1-891868-24-5
1. Bka'-gdams-pa (Sect)—Doctrines. 2. Atisa, 982-1054.
Bodhisattvamanyavali. I. Cameron, Ailsa. II. Title.
BQ7670.4.T48 2010
294.3'420423--dc22
2009048745
ISBN 978-1-891868-24-5

10 9 8 7 6 5 4 3 2 1

Cover photographer unknown
Cover line art by Robert Beer
Designed by Gopa & Ted2 Inc.

❂ Printed in the USA with environmental mindfulness on 30% PCW
recycled paper. The following resources have been saved: 55 trees, 1,542 lbs.
of solid waste, 25,403 gallons of water, 5,275 lbs. of greenhouse gases
and 18 million BTUs of energy.

Please contact the LAMA YESHE WISDOM ARCHIVE for more copies
of this and our other free books

···Contents···

APPENDIXES

· · · Benefactor's Dedication · · ·

IN LOVING MEMORY of our precious mother, Chin-Yu Wang Lai, who dedicated her life to supporting our father and nurturing six daughters with love and a natural ease. She possessed a spirit of generosity, strength in perseverance and a lighthearted sense of fun. She lived a full life that was filled with kindness and concern for others. Although she was unpretentious and modest about her accomplishments, Mom was a talented artist, an instinctive healer, a great cook and an adroit household manager. Last but not least, she was an entertaining storyteller. Her practical wisdom, warmth and humor touched lives that spanned across cultures and generations. We are blessed to have had her as our mother in this life.

May all kind mother sentient beings always be filled with joy and quickly actualize the path to ultimate happiness. May His Holiness the Dalai Lama, Lama Zopa Rinpoche and all glorious gurus have a long and stable life, and may all their holy wishes succeed immediately.

— *Lai Family*

··· Publisher's Acknowledgments ···

WE ARE EXTREMELY grateful to our friends and supporters who have made it possible for the LAMA YESHE WISDOM ARCHIVE to both exist and function: to Lama Yeshe and Lama Zopa Rinpoche, whose kindness is impossible to repay; to Peter and Nicole Kedge and Venerable Ailsa Cameron for their initial work on the ARCHIVE; to Venerable Roger Kunsang, Lama Zopa's tireless assistant, for his kindness and consideration; and to our sustaining supporters: Barry and Connie Hershey, Joan Halsall, Tony Steel, Vajrayana Institute, Claire Atkins, Thubten Yeshe, Roger and Claire Ash-Wheeler, Richard Gere, Doren and Mary Harper, Tom and Suzanne Castles, Lily Chang Wu and Hawk Furman.

Once again, we thank Ven. Ailsa Cameron for her expert and dedicated editing of Lama Zopa Rinpoche's most precious teachings.

We are also deeply grateful to all those who have become members of the ARCHIVE over the past few years. Details of our membership program may be found at the back of this book, and if you are not a member, please do consider joining up. Due to the kindness of those who have, we now have several editors working on our vast collection of teachings for the benefit of all. We have posted our list of individual and corporate members on our website, www.LamaYeshe.com.

In particular, we thank the Lai family for so kindly sponsoring
the production of this book in memory of their late mother, Chin-
Yu Wang Lai, for her sake and for that of all sentient beings. Lama
Zopa Rinpoche has said that sponsoring the publication of Dharma
teachings in memory of deceased relatives and friends was very
common in Tibet and is of great benefit. Therefore we encourage
others who might like to make Dharma books available for free distribution in this way to contact us for more information. Thank you
so much.

We also thank all the other kind people who contributed funds so
that we could print extra copies of this book.

Furthermore, we would like to express our appreciation for the
kindness and compassion of all those other generous benefactors
who have contributed funds to our work since we began publishing free books. Thankfully, you are too numerous to mention indi-
vidually in this book, but we value highly each and every donation
made to spreading the Dharma for the sake of the kind mother sentient beings and now pay tribute to you all on our website. Thank
you so much.

Finally, I would like to thank the many other kind people who
have asked that their donations be kept anonymous; my wife,
Wendy Cook, for her constant help and support; our dedicated
office staff, Jennifer Barlow and Ven. Ani Tenzin Desal; Ven. Ailsa
Cameron for her decades of meticulous editing; Ven. Connie Miller,
Gordon McDougall, Michelle Bernard and our other editors; Ven.
Kunsang for his tireless work recording Lama Zopa Rinpoche; Ven.
Thubten Labdron, Ven. Thubten Munsel and Dr. Su Hung for their

help with transcribing; Sandy Smith, Kim Li and our team of volunteer web editors; Ven. Bob Alcorn for his incredible work on our Lama Yeshe DVDs; David Zinn for his digital imaging expertise; Jonathan Steyn for his help with our audio work; Mandala Books and Wisdom Books for their great help with our distribution in Australia and Europe; and everybody else who helps us in so many ways. Thank you all.

If you, dear reader, would like to join this noble group of openhearted altruists by contributing to the production of more books by Lama Yeshe or Lama Zopa Rinpoche or to any other aspect of the Lama Yeshe Wisdom Archive's work, please contact us to find out how.

—*Dr. Nicholas Ribush*

Through the merit of having contributed to the spread of the Buddha's
teachings for the sake of all sentient beings, may our benefactors
and their families and friends have long and healthy lives,
all happiness, and may all their Dharma
wishes be instantly fulfilled.

· · · · ·

··· Editor's Preface ···

IN 1999 Lama Zopa Rinpoche asked Trisha Donnelly (now Venerable Thubten Labdron), the director of Root Institute, the FPMT[1] center in Bodhgaya, India, to obtain statues of Lama Atisha, Dromtönpa, Geshe Potowa, Geshe Langri Tangpa and Geshe Chekawa. The beautiful life-size statues, made in Nepal, were installed in the Root Institute gompa in 2000 and have subsequently been blessed by both His Holiness the Dalai Lama and His Holiness Karmapa. While statues of Lama Atisha are often seen, it is unusual to see statues of the Kadampa geshes.

In January 2003, in the presence of this unique collection of statues, Rinpoche explained that he wished to go over the life stories and teachings of the Kadampa geshes. While he gave teachings on various other subjects during this visit,[2] Rinpoche gave only a brief commentary to a verse of advice from the Kadampas and the oral transmissions of Lama Atisha's *Lamp of the Path to Enlightenment*, *Thought Transformation Eliminating Obstacles* and Geshe Langri Tangpa's *Eight Verses of Thought Transformation*.

---

[1] The Foundation for the Preservation of the Mahayana Traditon is the Dharma organization founded by Lama Yeshe and Lama Zopa Rinpoche.
[2] See Lama Yeshe Wisdom Archive number 1404.

On his return to Root Institute in December 2003, after giving a little of Lama Atisha's life story, Rinpoche proceeded to give the oral transmission of Lama Atisha's *The Bodhisattva's Jewel Garland* and an extensive commentary to its first two verses that also incorporated advice from Lama Tsongkhapa, Geshe Kharak Gomchung, Geshe Langri Tangpa and others.[3]

While Rinpoche did not teach on the Kadampas during the Maitreya Buddha retreat held at Root Institute in December 2005, he did give further commentary to *The Bodhisattva's Jewel Garland* in December 2006, again concentrating on the first two verses and incorporating advice from Shantideva, Geshe Kharak Gomchung, Geshe Langri Tangpa and others.[4]

In December 2007, after several discourses on the prayers preliminary to Dharma discourses,[5] in his final teaching Rinpoche returned to the topic of Kadampa teachings in relation to Kachen Yeshe Gyaltsen's *The Heart Advice of the Kadam Teachings: A Fine Vase of Nectar.* However, the mention of Kachen Yeshe Gyaltsen reminded Rinpoche of how he was inspired to teach the Kopan courses by Kachen Yeshe Gyaltsen's text *Great Thought Transformation.* After a long story about how he came to obtain the text, with detours through Solu Khumbu, Tibet and India, Rinpoche had time to give only the oral transmission of the first chapter of *The Heart Advice of the Kadam Teachings.* However, a couple of days later, prior to a Chenrezig Initiation, Rinpoche taught briefly on the guru devotion section of the

---

[3] LYWA #1470.
[4] LYWA #1588.
[5] LYWA #1683.

first chapter of *The Heart Advice of the Kadam Teachings* and extensively on dependent arising and emptiness.[6]

This book—very much a work in progress—is published with the hope that it creates the cause for Rinpoche to continue his teachings on the Kadampas at Root Institute and that it eventually forms part of a comprehensive volume of Rinpoche's commentaries to many more Kadampa teachings.

My thanks to Ven. Wy Ostenfeld for transcribing the 2007 teachings; to Geshe Lobsang Jamyang and Yaki Platt for their help with the Tibetan terms; to Nick Ribush and all the other dedicated workers at LYWA for their support; to all the Root Institute directors, spiritual program coordinators and audio people for organizing and recording the teachings included in this book; and to Claire Atkins and Ven. Lhagsam for their continued generous support.

[6] LYWA #1677.

Lama Zopa Rinpoche at Root Institute.

Todd Moore

Kadampa Teachings 1

BODHGAYA, JANUARY 2003

Lama Atisha (Dipamkara Shrijnana), 982–1054

Jerry Powers

··· Kadampa Teachings 1 ···

January 24

GOOD AFTERNOON EVERYONE. A few years ago I advised Root Institute to have some Kadampa statues made, and there are now statues of Lama Atisha and the Kadampa lamas: Dromtönpa; Geshe Potowa; Geshe Langri Tangpa, who composed *The Eight Verses of Thought Transformation*; and Geshe Chekawa, whose teaching, *The Seven Points of Thought Transformation*, is very commonly taught everywhere, in the East as well as in the West.

There are statues that you commonly see in monasteries and meditation centers, but you don't normally see statues of the Kadampa lamas, even though their teachings are often taught and also mentioned in Lama Tsongkhapa's *The Great Treatise on the Stages of the Path to Enlightenment*, as well as in *Liberation in the Palm of Your Hand* and many other lam-rim teachings. I thought it would be very good to have statues of these Kadampa lamas, great Tibetan meditators who attained the path and whose teachings, which we read and study, express their own experiences during their many years of practice, when they sacrificed themselves to experiment on the path.

The purpose of having the statues of these great Kadampa geshes is to pray to them to develop devotion and to rejoice in their attainments and in the extensive benefit they have brought sentient beings in this world, including us, and all other sentient beings. We are very fortunate to be able to see the statues of their holy bodies, which remind us of how they practiced Dharma, particularly bodhicitta, the good heart, letting go of the I and cherishing others. Since we have these precious statues, my wish is to go over their life stories, the stories of how they practiced and of how they benefited sentient beings and the teaching of the Buddha, to inspire us to be like them and to rejoice in their activities.

• • •

The Kadampa geshes give three pieces of advice on how to go about the path to full enlightenment. (I'm supposed to be giving teachings on the Kadampas, so I've finally come to some words of the Kadampas.)[7]

> Look far ahead.
> Generate a vast mind.
> Don't squeeze yourself.

I don't remember which Kadampa geshe said this[8]—it's mentioned in the Kadampa thought-transformation teachings and also as a conclusion at the end of Pabongka Dechen Nyingpo's commentary to The Three Principles of the Path.

[7] Rinpoche has returned to the subject of the Kadampas after a long discourse on many other subjects.
[8] Pabongka Rinpoche attributes this quote to Geshe Kharak Gomchung in Liberation in the Palm of Your Hand and to Geshe Dolpa in his commentary to The Three Principles of the Path (see The Principal Teachings of Buddhism, p. 139 and note 174, p. 190). Others attribute it to Gompa Rinchen Lama.

The first piece of advice is *mig gyang zig*, or *Look far ahead*. Since your objective is to achieve enlightenment, you have to look far ahead, just as when you're traveling to somewhere very distant, you have to generate a strong determination to go there.

The second advice is *lo gya kye*, or *Generate a vast mind*. For example, you could be a small child in kindergarten, but your final objective might be gaining a university degree. You have to look far ahead and generate a vast mind, thinking that you are going to do all the preliminary study in primary school and high school and finally study in university and get your degree. With a broad mind, a vast mind, you make a plan to study all these things.

The third advice is *kong sang lhö*, or *Don't squeeze yourself*. Don't allow yourself to become stressed out, thinking, "Oh, I have to do all this!" With a vast, brave mind, think, "I'm going to do all this. Even if it takes many, many years, I'm going to do it." When you do follow the advice, *Don't squeeze yourself*, your mind naturally relaxes. Your mind is not stressed, not uptight, which causes *lung*, or wind disease. I think the new people here don't know about lung, but you'll soon be introduced to it.

You should have a vast mind, planning to study and learn everything about the whole path to enlightenment, as well as to practice it and actualize all the realizations. While you have that plan, you also have a relaxed mind; you don't stress yourself. You think, "No matter how long it takes, I'm going to do it. I'm not going to give up." You have the plan inside your heart, but at the same time your mind is calm and relaxed.

These are essential pieces of advice from the Kadampa geshes about how to go about achieving enlightenment. And if you follow these instructions you will definitely achieve enlightenment, even though you might think it's impossible. You might think, "I can see that I have many delusions. My mind is like a garbage can completely filled with garbage or like a septic tank completely filled with excrement, gas and other stuff. Since my mind is filled with all these negative emotional thoughts, how can I become an enlightened being? How can I even generate bodhicitta? It's not possible for me to completely let go of the I and only cherish and benefit others!" Because at the moment the only thing you see in your heart is self-cherishing, the wish to do everything for your own benefit day and night, you think, "How's it possible for me to change my mind into only cherishing others, only benefiting others?" However, if you follow the Kadampa geshes' advice and learn Dharma and practice it correctly, it will happen, even though you now believe it's impossible. As Kadampa Geshe Dölpa said:

> If you collect merit, purify your obstacles and practice
> guru devotion, which causes you to receive blessings in
> your heart, and put effort into meditating on the path,
> even the difficult realizations you believe won't happen
> will happen within a few years.[9]

This can happen because your present mind is only temporarily obscured; your obscurations are not oneness with your mind. All

[9] This passage is cited in both *The Great Treatise on the Stages of the Path to Enlightenment* and *Liberation in the Palm of Your Hand.*

your negative emotional thoughts are temporary, not permanent. Since they happened because of causes and conditions, they can be changed by other causes and conditions, by purifying negativities, collecting merit, practicing guru devotion and meditating on the path. With a long-term plan to learn and to practice Dharma, your mind can completely change, and you can achieve realizations.

January 27
LAMP OF THE PATH TO ENLIGHTENMENT

Lamp of the Path to Enlightenment is the root text composed by Lama Atisha.[10] I didn't get to go over Lama Atisha's life story, even though that was my wish; but since many of you have read *Liberation in the Palm of Your Hand*, you already have an idea of who Lama Atisha is, of all his qualities and his incredible benefit to sentient beings, including those in this world. Every day, whenever we meditate on lam-rim or go over a lam-rim prayer, Lama Atisha is helping us. Even the term *lam-rim* came only after Lama Atisha had composed *Lamp of the Path to Enlightenment*. Before that there was no such text that condensed the whole 84,000 teachings of Buddha, the teachings of the Hinayana, Paramitayana and Mahayana tantric paths, and that was set up as one person's graduated practice to achieve enlightenment. There was no such thing that enabled one, easily and without confusion, to go about achieving enlightenment. Nothing else was so clearly arranged. Even though the vast volumes of the *Kangyur* and

---

[10] The text may be found in *Illuminating the Path to Enlightenment* or online at www.LamaYeshe.com.

Tengyur contained the subjects of the whole path to enlightenment, there was no integration of the subject material. Lama Atisha made it unbelievably easy for us sentient beings to practice; he taught us how to go about achieving enlightenment in accordance with the level, or capacity, of our own mind. He made the way to follow the path to enlightenment very clear and very easy.

Every day when we read a lam-rim prayer as a direct meditation or meditate on lam-rim, we plant seeds of the whole path to enlightenment, and each day we become closer and closer to enlightenment. Each time we meditate on lam-rim we become closer to the realizations of the path and to enlightenment, and this is by Lama Atisha's kindness, which is as limitless as the sky. The benefit he has brought us—our lives, our hearts, our minds—is like the limitless sky. No words can express the kindness of Lama Atisha in this degenerate time.

Somebody requested me to give the oral transmission of *Lamp of the Path to Enlightenment*. The oral transmission can be given in English if it's a correct translation; but if the translation isn't correct, you can miss some of the words. Since everything in the Tibetan might not be there in the English, it might be safer to do the oral transmission in Tibetan.

Think that you will listen to the oral transmission for the benefit of all sentient beings and then think, "May each word that I listen to immediately cause me to have realization. May the effect of each word on my mental continuum be to liberate me from the oceans of samsaric suffering and its cause, karma and delusion. May each word be like an atomic bomb on the sufferings of samsara."

Each word of Dharma, of lam-rim, has that power to affect your mental continuum. If you think in this way you can then see the value of each Dharma word you hear; you can see how precious each word is. It also helps you to pay attention to the words, to put all your effort into listening so that you don't miss any words. Understanding the benefits encourages you.

Then think, "May each word of Dharma that I listen to enable me to benefit all sentient beings." When we are about to listen to a teaching, it's very good to pray like this at the beginning.

Also think, "When I then teach on this text, may each word of Dharma cause realizations of the path to be immediately actualized in sentient beings' hearts." If we dedicate in this way, it can then happen, because of the power of mind, the power of prayer.

[Rinpoche gives the oral transmission of *Lamp of the Path to Enlightenment* in Tibetan.]

THOUGHT TRANSFORMATION ELIMINATING OBSTACLES

This is a short teaching called *Thought Transformation Eliminating Obstacles*, which we can use to deal with obstacles in our daily life. (See appendix 1.) I'm not sure which lama composed it. There are a few other pieces of advice, but it doesn't say who wrote them. However, at the end of one of the teachings, it says it was composed by Pel Narthang Khenpo, the abbot of Narthang Monastery. On the road from the Nepalese border to Lhasa, you pass through Narthang before you arrive in Shigatse. It's one of the places where the *Kangyur* and *Tengyur* are printed and where original wood blocks for them are kept. I heard that during the Cultural Revolution all the wood blocks and many unbelievably precious teachings were piled up in a field and burned. It took them weeks and weeks to burn everything. I also heard that rainbows came from that site. Wood blocks of the *Kangyur* and *Tengyur* were kept and printed at three places in Tibet: Narthang, Lhasa and Derge. There are editions of the *Kangyur* and *Tengyur* according to Narthang, Lhasa and Derge.

I'm not completely sure, but this teaching might have been composed by Chim Namkha Drak, the abbot of Narthang Monastery.[11]

I prostrate to Guru Compassionate One.

The Mahayana thought transformation eliminating obstacles means taking inauspicious signs as good fortune....

Ordinary people, thinking that an inauspicious sign is bad, become so worried and upset that they then have mos[12] and pujas done. But a practitioner of thought transformation uses any inauspicious sign, any bad omen, that happens in their life to destroy the ego, the self-cherishing thought, and to develop bodhicitta and achieve enlightenment to be able to enlighten other sentient beings. For them, the inauspicious sign becomes good luck.

I will read the text quickly in Tibetan.

[Rinpoche gives the oral transmission of *Thought Transformation Eliminating Obstacles* in Tibetan.]

[11] Thupten Jinpa attributes the authorship to Shönu Gyalchok. See note 367 in *Mind Training: The Great Collection*.
[12] The Tibetan word *mo* means a divination in reliance upon a meditational deity, usually performed with dice.

THE EIGHT VERSES OF THOUGHT TRANSFORMATION

I was also requested to give the oral transmission of *The Eight Verses of Thought Transformation* by someone who said that they were going to practice it in their life, which means use it to benefit all sentient beings. *The Eight Verses* was composed by Kadampa Geshe Langri Tangpa, whose statue is here in the Root Institute gompa.[13]

[Rinpoche gives the oral transmission of *The Eight Verses of Thought Transformation* in Tibetan.]

[13] See *Teachings from Tibet*, pp. 159-179, for the root text and a short commentary by His Holiness the Dalai Lama.

Lama Dromtönpa (Gyalwai Jungné) 1005–64

Jerry Powers

Kadampa Teachings 2

BODHGAYA, DECEMBER 2003–JANUARY 2004

Geshe Potowa (Rinchen Sal) 1027–1105

Jerry Powers

···Kadampa Teachings 2···

December 27

I THOUGHT TO READ a little bit of Lama Atisha's life story, since the root of the lam-rim teaching is Lama Atisha's *Lamp of the Path to Enlightenment*.

I requested that Root Institute have the statues of these Kadampa geshes. Seeing these statues inspires you to practice lam-rim and transform your mind into the path and particularly to practice *lo-jong*, or thought transformation, which means using obstacles to practice Dharma. As the Kadampa geshes did, you can use any undesirable thing that you experience—a strong delusion arising, sickness, an obstacle to your Dharma practice—in the path to achieve enlightenment. You can use even your delusions, your negative thoughts, in the path to achieve enlightenment for sentient beings. When ignorance, anger, attachment or self-cherishing arises strongly, you can do *tong-len*, taking and giving, in which you take all the delusions of other sentient beings into your own heart and give them to your self-cherishing thought, thus destroying it. When there's strong attachment, you take the attachment of all sentient beings within yourself and use it to destroy your attachment.

You use all the undesirable things, all the obstacles to practicing

Dharma, transforming them all into the path to enlightenment. Taking all the similar problems of the numberless sentient beings, all the sufferings and delusions, upon yourself is like transforming poison into medicine. Instead of harming your health, the poison then becomes beneficial for your health. You use what is regarded as an obstacle to practicing Dharma to develop bodhicitta or to meditate on emptiness. By taking all those obstacles, all those problems, of other sentient beings on yourself, giving all of them to your self-cherishing thought, you will have no obstacles to your practice of Dharma. When you use obstacles to practice thought transformation or lam-rim and bring happiness to all sentient beings, you'll have no obstacles to your Dharma practice. Before there were obstacles to your Dharma practice; but after you have applied the meditation of thought transformation, you won't find any obstacles to your practice. Since the Kadampa geshes whose statues are here did this practice, they inspire us to practice lam-rim, the heart of the 84,000 teachings of Buddha, and to transform all our sufferings, all our obstacles, into happiness, into the path to enlightenment, thus becoming the cause of happiness for all sentient beings.

LAMA ATISHA'S LIFE STORY

Rather than reading Lama Atisha's life story from the Tibetan, it might be quicker for me to read the English.[14] This is to inspire devo-

---

[14] Rinpoche read the following excerpt from *Atisha: A Biography of the Renowned Buddhist Sage*, translated by Lama Thubten Kalsang et al., which may be found at LamaYeshe.com.

tion to Lama Atisha. The lam-rim, the special way of presenting the Dharma, came from Lama Atisha. When other teachings can't subdue the mind, the lam-rim is the only one that can.

> In the eastern part of India, in the country named Bengal (Sahor), the ruler was a religious king named Kalyana Shri. King Kalyana Shri brought the prosperity of his kingdom to its zenith. His palace had a golden victory banner encircled by countless houses and there were great numbers of bathing-pools encircled by 720 magnificent gardens, forests of Tala trees, seven concentric walls, 363 connecting bridges, innumerable golden victory banners, thirteen roofs to the central palace and thousands of noblemen in the palace.

> All this splendor matched the King of Tonkun's (one of the Chinese kings); the dignity of the monarch's royal bearing and his air of great authority were like those of the great god Indra. His subjects were as numerous as the inhabitants of a city of Gandharas and their religious attainments could be compared to those of Aryadharma. Shri Prabhavati, the consort of this devout king, was like a goddess. She was a beautiful and chaste woman who worshipped the Triple Gem, and was beloved as a mother by all human beings. This queen had three sons, namely Shrigarbha, Chandragarbha and Padmagarbha. The story of these three is seldom to be found in other books. The second son, Chandragarbha, was my noble guru. At the

auspicious moment of his birth, flowers rained down upon the city, a rainbow canopy appeared, and the gods sang hymns which brought gladness and joy to all the people. For eighteen months he resided in the capital and was excellently reared by eight nurses.

To the north of the palace there was a sacred place called Vikramshila Vihara. To make offerings at that place, the King, Queen and their ministers, escorted by 500 chariots full of lovely girls elegantly adorned with ornaments and surrounded by hundreds upon hundreds of musicians, carried the innumerable jeweled articles necessary for the votive rite and all went to that place singing.

My infant guru, who already seemed like a child of three, had so many beauties of person that the eyes were dazzled. The boy, having been crowned and adorned with god-like ornaments, was carried by his father wrapped in fine muslin garments. When the people saw him they felt so full of happiness that they could not tear themselves away. Those who stood by exclaimed: "At the time of your birth, the tent of the sun was set up and melodious songs were heard by the people. So our most cherished desire was to meet you. And now, having seen you, we are filled with joyous awe."

I don't remember seeing this story before. In the Tibetan text it says that all these things were arranged by the king and queen, Atisha's father and mother, so that the prince, Atisha, would be impressed, or *dazzled*, as it says here. They chose many beautiful girls and an extensive range of songs to make staying home more attractive to Atisha than going away from home to become a monk. I don't remember seeing this story in the Tibetan text, but the text with the stories of the lam-rim lineage lamas mentions what his parents prayed for and the prayer that Lama Atisha made when his parents made all these extensive arrangements to try to get him to stay at home.

> Then the excellent Prince enquired:
> "Who are these people, O parents?"
> "These are your subjects, Prince," answered his parents.
> Then the excellent Prince continued: "May they be possessed of merit like that of my parents. May they rule kingdoms that reach the summit of prosperity. May they be reborn as sons of kings and may they be sustained by holy and virtuous deeds."
>
> Then, when the royal procession came safely to the Vikramashila Vihara (the main chapel at that place of pilgrimage) the excellent Prince, having prostrated himself to the Triple Gem, recited this melodious song of praise: "Having attained the noble body of a man, and being without defect in all organs, I shall adhere to the Triple Gem.
>
> Always, I shall take the Triple Gem upon my head with deep sincerity.
> Henceforward, may the Triple Gem be my refuge!"

When these words were heard by the King, Queen, ministers and monks, they were filled with joyful wonder and all declared with one voice that the Prince was destined for greatness. Then the King, Queen and attendants declared: "May we, by gathering merits through paying reverence and making offerings, be able to make offerings to the Triple Gem from life to life. And, by the virtue of those merits, we pray for the long continuance of our religion, for which we shall make offerings to the Sangha. Oh, may we be delivered from the sufferings caused by defilements."

When the Prince heard their words, he looked at his parents and exclaimed: "May I never be bound by worldly ways. May I be taught the holy way of the monks and humbly worship the Triple Gem. May I feel pity for all beings."

I'm not sure that *pity* is the right word—maybe *compassion* would be better.

"May I feel compassion for all living beings."

His parents and the others felt full of wonder when they heard the sayings of the Prince. This was the first preaching of my guru.

So, this was the first teaching from Lama Atisha.

The Prince, by the age of three, had become well-versed in astrology, writing and Sanskrit. At six years, he was able to

distinguish between the Buddhist and non-Buddhist doctrines. From then up to the age of ten years, he took the
Triple Gem for refuge by observing the precepts (*shilas*) of
the *upasakas*, bestowing charity (*dana*), studying happily,
reciting prayers, seeking out people of noble character,
obeying and serving his parents humbly and with sweet
words, enjoying every sort of religious dance and sacred
song, paying respect to holy men even from a distance,
looking at worldlings with heart-felt pity, helping those
who were wretched, and doing many such noble deeds.
When the Prince reached the age of eleven years, the ministers and subjects brought twenty-one girls of noble par-
entage to him and the King and Queen presented them
with valuable gifts.

One day the King summoned all his ministers and com-
manded: "Beginning from tomorrow you must carefully
prepare the thirteen royal chariots and adorn them beautifully with innumerable ornaments such as the people
love, especially the most beautiful and strongest chariot,
which should be placed in the center. On it you must pitch
the peacock umbrella surrounded by fans. In the center
(under the peacock umbrella) place Chandragarbha clad
in splendid garments on a beautifully jeweled throne. In
the other twelve adorned chariots, all the ministers will be
seated dressed in magnificent garments and accompanied
by musicians with many kinds of instruments to play joyful songs.

"The procession will be led by three white chariots; there will be three red chariots to the rear, three yellow chariots on the right and three green chariots on the left. In each of the chariots place many youths and maidens with colored banners proper to the devas of the four directions. The Prince's chariot of five different colors should be ornamented at the four corners with carvings shaped like peacocks' necks and surrounded by girls dressed as goddesses bearing offerings. The other attendants should play melodious tunes upon such instruments as violins, drums and cymbals to delight the crowds who will gather on all sides. Beyond the great city in a pleasant garden must be set all sorts of amusements and games that will draw the people to assemble there. These amusements must last for a period of half a month so as to make all the people happy and contented. Among the assembly, there must be girls ready to delight the Prince, and the ministers must instruct them how to behave when the Prince's gaze lights upon them."

Thus the great king ordered the ministers to get ready thirteen adorned chariots within a week, with the chariot of the Prince in the middle, richly ornamented, and twelve chariots of musicians with instruments of all sorts.

Then beyond the great city at all the crossroads and in the gardens, the people began enjoying themselves with fascinating games. During the royal progress through all the quarters of the city to which Prince Chandragarbha and his 25,000 attendants proceeded in their chariots, the people in the lotus gardens adjacent to the capital and at every junction of the roads welcomed him like a universal king (*chakravartin*) and all followed to gaze at the Prince. Prabhadevi and the other court ladies, the Prince's kinsmen and comrades, encouraged one another to hasten to see the gathering of people. When the people came crowding around the procession, the daughters of King Punnadhara, King Nemandhara, King Jalapati, King Pracandraprabha and other kings of high descent, noble physique and great possessions came armed, riding in twenty-two chariots, to join in the celebrations. In each of the chariots rode seven girls with seven maiden attendants. All these twenty-two chariots were adorned magnificently with diverse ornaments. The riders came singing melodious songs and in happy mood. The girls sat like goddesses, their lovelorn eyes fixed upon the Prince, for, at the sight of this youth, their passion was so great that the hair on their limbs stood up.

Suddenly, a goddess appeared, her complexion pale blue, and uttered the following admonition to the Prince: "O, care not for power and be free from lust, most fortunate Prince.

If, as an elephant sinks deeply into the swamp, you, a hero,
    were to sink in the mire of lust,
Would it not stain the shila robes you have worn

In your past five hundred and fifty-two lives

When you took the form of an undefiled *pandita*, a holy

bhikshu?

Therefore, as ducks seek out the lotus garden,

Seek you ordination in this life.

The charming and lovely girls who live in this city

Are temptresses sent by *mara* (the evil one) to dispel your

brilliant shila,

Thus they hope to betray you by showing you their passion.

Know this, O handsome Prince!

Like the moon reflected in the ocean,

Your purity gives forth brilliance, O Prince.

Your head adorned with the five sacred jeweled ornaments

Puts a spell of fascination upon the people.

Since you have attained a precious human body, so difficult to

win,

You should devote your life to hearing, pondering and

practicing (the Dharma)

And, to set your doubts at rest,

You should seek the guidance of innumerable gurus."

The Prince smiled and responded thus to the goddess's
admonition:

"Oh, wonderful! This is good, this is good, most excellently

good!

The wise delight in the (silence of the) forest,

As peacocks thrive on poisonous plants

Or as ducks rejoice in the water of the lake.

Just as crows revel in dirty places,

So do ordinary people flock to the city.

Whereas, like ducks hastening to the lotus pond,

Do people of wisdom seek the forest.

How unlike ordinary people!

So, in the past, was Prince Siddhartha

Repelled by the prosperous kingdom of Shuddhodana as by a
    filthy swamp.

He thereupon sought enlightenment, renouncing all his royal
    consorts.

All humans and devas praised and worshipped him.

Possessing the thirty-two glorious signs and eighty noble
    marks of a Dharma king,

He attained buddhahood attended by the twelve holy states.

Unless I renounce this kingdom,

I shall increase the lust in the swamp of evil.

All friends are deceivers sent by mara.

All wealth is but a salty river.

Now by seeking eminent gurus

And by making good use of this body, I shall attain
    enlightenment.

The enjoyment of pleasures stemming from desire

Is as empty as reflected moonlight,

As fleeting as an echo,

As illusory as a mirage,

As dependent as a reflection.

Into this vast ocean of affliction,

The rivers of birth, decay, sickness and death flow

    unceasingly.

In the past, I was bound by the karmic power of impure

    deeds,

But today I am able to fulfill this life, so why not seek after

    Dharma?

Determined to seek deliverance from worldly things,

I shall devote myself to the noble Dharma under the guidance

    of my gurus."

I will now give the oral transmission of a short teaching by Lama Atisha, *The Bodhisattva's Jewel Garland*.

Think, "The purpose of my life is to free the numberless sentient beings from all their suffering and its causes and bring them to enlightenment; therefore, I must achieve enlightenment; and therefore, I'm going to take the oral transmission of Lama Atisha's teaching, *The Bodhisattva's Jewel Garland*."

[Rinpoche gives the oral transmission of *The Bodhisattva's Jewel Garland* in Tibetan.]

I received the oral transmission of *The Bodhisattva's Jewel Garland* from Kirti Tsenshab Rinpoche in Dharamsala quite a number of years ago. I requested Rinpoche to give the oral transmission of the many thought-transformation texts compiled by the great bodhisattva Konchog Gyaltsen.[15] I received all those teachings except

---

[15] This is *Mind Training: The Great Collection* op cit.

for *Parting from the Four Clingings*, composed by the great Sakya lama, Dragpa Gyaltsen, as Rinpoche didn't hold that lineage. I later received that teaching, as well as the commentaries to it, in Nepal from His Holiness Chogye Trichen Rinpoche.

December 28

To keep our mind in Dharma and always strongly devoted to Dharma, to be inspired to do pure Dharma practice and to receive blessings, it's very good to read the life stories of Dharma practitioners such as the Kadampa geshes, Milarepa and Lama Tsongkhapa. Read whatever is available in your language. Reading the life stories of those who have attained the path inspires your mind, causing you to develop devotion and to receive blessings. Also, by reading the life stories of highly attained great yogis and pandits, or scholars, you know how to practice Dharma.

When we read the life story of Milarepa or Lama Atisha and generate a wish to be like them, we are making preparation in our mental continuum to be like them in the future, sooner or later. Generating a strong wish to be like them is a positive wish, and from that wish we then become like them, with all those qualities, and are able to offer extensive benefit to sentient beings. While you are reading their life stories, pray again and again to be like them. Put your palms together and recite the verse:

> Päl dän la ma khye ku chi dra dang
> Khor dang ku tshei tshä dang zhing kham sog

Khyö kyi tshän chhog zang po chi dra war

De dra kho nar dag sog gyur war shog

In whatever way you appear, glorious guru,

With whatever retinue, life span and pure land,

Whatever noble and holy name you take,

May I and others attain only these.

· · ·

I mentioned the importance of reading the life stories of the lineage lamas of the lam-rim path, those great yogis who completed the path. We should read the life stories of present yogis and of the ancient ones, those who accomplished the path, so that we come to know how to practice Dharma. It's one way of subduing our mind, of softening the concrete concepts of our heavy mind. It is only then that realizations can come.

If we pray in this way whenever we see these statues of the Kadampa geshes in the Root Institute gompa, for example, sooner or later we will become like them. We will have all those qualities and be able to practice Dharma and benefit so many sentient beings as Lama Atisha and the Kadampa geshes did. Every time we come into the gompa and see these statues and the other holy objects, it's very important that we immediately put our hands together in prostration. We should take all the advantages offered by these statues and holy objects. They are here for us sentient beings to collect merit and to purify our defilements and obstacles and to achieve realizations of the path. They are here for us to achieve liberation from samsara and full enlightenment. We must take every opportunity we have to use these holy objects to collect merit and to purify our mind. We must pray to be like them, so that sooner or later, by the power of our mind, by the power of our wish, or intention, we can become like them. As mentioned in the teachings, "All phenomena depend on the tip of a wish."

Remember the story of Shariputra, Guru Shakyamuni Buddha's heart disciple. As mentioned by the great Pabongka Dechen Nyingpo in *Liberation in the Palm of Your Hand*, the reason that Shariputra was able to be Buddha's heart disciple and always be with Buddha was because of what happened in one of his past lives. While traveling, he stopped overnight in a temple. He was fixing his shoes by a light, facing a wall. He would sometimes take a rest and gaze at a drawing of a buddha on the wall. Each time he looked at the drawing he thought, "How beautiful it is!" He generated the wish, the positive intention, to become like that. That is why Shariputra was able to become the heart disciple of Guru Shakyamuni Buddha and always see, serve and receive teachings from Buddha.

THE BODHISATTVA'S JEWEL GARLAND

In the Indian language, Sanskrit, this text is called *Bodhisattvamanevali*; in Tibetan, *jang chub sem pai nor bu treng wa*; and in the English language, *The Bodhisattva's Jewel Garland*.

I prostrate to great compassion;

I prostrate to the gurus;

I prostrate to the devotional deities.

Abandon all doubts;

Definitely cherish the practice.

Here it says *Abandon all doubts*, but how do we do this? In one way, as we learn more, we're able to cut doubts. The more we study Dharma, the deeper our learning, the fewer doubts we have.

However, intellectual learning alone is not enough to really cut doubts. We must practice and purify our defilements. Otherwise, if we don't purify our mind, even if we have good intellectual understanding of what is said in the texts or explained by our teachers, doubts will come. While we're doing preliminary practices—while we're prostrating to Buddha, for example—doubts can sometimes come. The thought can come, "There's no Buddha" or "There's no reincarnation" or "There's no karma." Such heretical thoughts can come, if only for a short time. Learning is one thing, but, from my point of view, the main thing is to purify defilements. This is how we can be free from doubts; this is how we can abandon doubts. Otherwise, we will have doubts about very simple things, not even sophisticated philosophical points. If we have thick obscurations, doubts can arise about even very simple things. Purification is important. Otherwise, even though we have faith in karma and so forth, some past negative imprint for heresy will manifest now and then, and our mind will totally change. When that happens, we are convinced that what we believed before is wrong. When a past negative imprint for heresy manifests, we can totally believe that there's no reincarnation, no karma, no liberation. Therefore, I think it's very important every day to do purification practice and to do prayers dedicating merits.

In the early times at Kopan, around the time of the third, fourth and fifth Kopan courses,[16] we would introduce the subjects of the mind and reincarnation then spend at least a few days talking about them. For four or five days, like many birds chattering in a tree, there would be a lot of discussion about the mind. It would be like that for a few days, then slowly calm down. After a week, everything would be quite calm. But even after two weeks, even though most people were fine, there would still be two or three people who couldn't understand reincarnation, who couldn't figure it out.

It has all to do with an individual person's karma. It's a question of obscurations. If someone's mind is impure and has thick obscurations, no matter how intelligent the logical reasoning you use is, you won't be able to prove the existence of reincarnation to that person. Even though other people accept your logic and say, "Of course, it's like that," that particular person won't accept reincarnation. It is only when that person does practice of purification that there can be a change.

Thoroughly abandon sleep, drowsiness and laziness.

This has come at the right time, the perfect time!

Always attempt to have perseverance.

Geshe Wangchen has done a translation of *The Bodhisattva's Jewel Garland*, though it's more an explanation of the meaning than a

---

[16] 1972–73

literal translation. (See appendix 2.)[17] Geshe Wangchen's translation here is:

> Having removed sleepiness, dullness and laziness,
> I shall always be joyful
> When engaging in such incredible practices.

PRACTICING MINDFULNESS

The next verse is:

> With remembrance, awareness and conscientiousness,
> Always protect the doors of your senses.
> Three times day and night, again and again,
> Examine your mental continuum

It means we must examine our mental continuum again and again: morning, noon, evening and night.

Here Geshe Wangchen's translation is:

> I shall guard the doors of my speech, body and mind
> Against any negative action,
> By constantly being alert and mindful in my behavior.
> I shall examine my mind
> Over and over again, day and night.

---

[17] Other translations of this text may be found in *Advice from a Spiritual Friend* and *The Book of Kadam*, p. 61.

We should practice mindfulness so that we are able to recognize whether or not negative thoughts are arising and whether or not we're engaging in negative actions. Mindfulness is the first thing, the foundation. Through mindfulness we can recognize whether there's a danger of our giving rise to anger, attachment, ignorance, self-cherishing or another delusion or of engaging in negative actions that will harm others and ourselves.

Mindfulness of impermanence

Sometimes, because there's no mindfulness, we engage in negative karma without recognizing it. That is due to ignorance. While causative phenomena such as our life and the objects of our senses are impermanent in nature, continuously changing, decaying, in every hour, every minute, every second, and can be stopped at any time, they appear to us to be permanent, and we let our mind believe that they're always going to be this way, which is the opposite to impermanence. Even though these things are impermanent in nature, we believe they're always going to be this way.

Mindfulness of emptiness

Things also exist in mere name, being merely labeled by the mind; they're dependent arisings, existing in mere name in dependence upon their base, the mind that labels them and their label. Even though that's how things exist, because there's the hallucination of a truly existent appearance, they don't appear to us in accord with the reality, as merely labeled by mind, but appear to be not merely labeled by mind. We have a hallucinated view, and when we then allow our mind to hold on to that view as true, at that time we are creating ignorance in our daily life. This ignorance is the basis, or root, of all other delusions, of all other negative emotional thoughts, which then motivate karma. Here we need to practice mindfulness so that instead of thinking that this view is true, we think the opposite, that things are merely labeled by mind. We need to practice mindfulness of subtle dependent arising.

This is how things exist, from the I, the general aggregates, each individual aggregate, down to the atoms of the body. According to the Prasangika school, all atoms are composed of particles; there's no atom that has no parts. An atom exists by being merely labeled on a collection of particles, which is then labeled on another collection of particles.

Just to give you some idea of this: the aggregate of form is not the I, the aggregate of feeling is not the I, the aggregate of recognition is not the I, the compositional factors are not the I, the aggregate of consciousness is not the I. Even the collection of all five of these aggregates is not the I. The I exists nowhere, from the top of the head down to the toes. It is not only that the truly existent I doesn't exist on the aggregates. You can't find even the labeled I on the aggregates, on the base. It doesn't mean that the I that is merely labeled doesn't exist. It exists. Even though you cannot find it on the base, the labeled I exists. The labeled I is in India, in Bodhgaya, in this gompa, on this cushion. It is on this cushion, but you can't find it on this base. It exists on this cushion while the aggregates are on this cushion. You can't find that labeled I on this base, but it is here now in this gompa, on this cushion, while the aggregates are on this cushion in this gompa. So, what is that I? It is nothing other than what is merely imputed by the mind.

The I doesn't exist as one with these aggregates, nor does it exist separately from them. There is no other concrete reason to prove that there's an I except that there is the valid base of the I, the aggregates. That's it. Because the base is there, this valid base receives the label "I." So, the mind has merely imputed "I."

Just because the base, the aggregates, is now in India, in Bodhgaya, in the Root Institute gompa, the mind has merely imputed "I" and believed "I am in India, in Bodhgaya, in the Root Institute gompa." Just because of that, the I is merely imputed, and we believe in that.

It is the same with everything else. When our body is doing the action of sitting, our mind merely imputes "I am sitting" and believes in that. There's nothing more than that. There's no I other than that. There's no I that is something real or something more than that. The I that appears to be more than that and that we believe to be more than that is a false I. That is what is empty.

According to what the mind, the speech or the body does, the mind merely imputes "I am doing this or that" and believes in that. Seeing what the base does, the mind merely labels the action and believes in that. It's not that there's no I, but when you compare how the I appeared to you before and how you believed it to be a real I existing from its own side with how the I appears with this present analysis, it's like the I doesn't exist. It's not that the I doesn't exist, but it's like it doesn't exist. It is not that it's totally nonexistent. It exists, but it's so subtle that it's like it doesn't exist. It is extremely fine, extremely subtle. You now have some idea of how the I is empty, empty of that real I that used to appear to you before and in which you believed.

You can't say that the I doesn't exist; it exists. But it's something unbelievably subtle. It is empty of that emotional I, that real I. While it is empty, it exists; it exists in mere name. So, this is how the I is— extremely subtle. When we analyze how the I exists, we find it's not what has been appearing to us and what we have been believing in from this morning, from our birth, from beginningless rebirths. It is never that I that we have been holding on to, thinking that it's true. That one has never existed; during beginningless rebirths that one has never existed. Such an I has never existed up to now. There's no such I. Even the omniscient mind cannot see that I. What the omniscient mind sees is that the I is empty of that. All those who have realized emptiness see that the I is empty of that; this is what they realize.

It is the same with each of the aggregates. Each aggregate is empty of the real one appearing from there that we believe is true. All the aggregates are empty, but they are not totally nonexistent. They exist, but they exist in mere name; they function in mere name. From the I down to the atoms and the particles of the atoms, everything is like that, merely labeled. Everything exists by being merely labeled; everything exists in mere name, merely labeled by the mind.

It is the same with the consciousness. This hour's consciousness, this minute's consciousness, this second's consciousness, this split-second's consciousness—they all exist in mere name, merely labeled by the mind. (The shortest duration of time varies with the different schools. For the Vaibhashika school, there are sixty-five moments in the duration of a finger-snap; for the Mahayana schools, there are 365.) However, down to the shortest duration of the continuity of consciousness, everything exists in mere name, merely labeled by the mind.

When you are sitting here, in reality there are all these piles of labels, from the I down to the particles of the atoms or the split-seconds of consciousness. One label is labeled on one thing, which is labeled on another thing. The I is labeled because there are the aggregates, and the aggregates are merely labeled because of the collection of the five aggregates. The aggregate of form is merely labeled because of the collection of all the parts of the body, and it is similar with the other aggregates. So, down to the particles of the atoms and the split-seconds of consciousness, everything exists in mere name, merely imputed by the mind. Every single part of what is sitting here is what has been merely imputed by the mind; it exists in mere name.

It is the same when you are walking. From the I down to the particles of the atoms and the split-seconds of consciousness, everything that is functioning exists in mere name. All the activities of the I are also merely labeled by the mind; they all exist in mere name.

When this analysis of the I is done, we get some experience of how the I exists. We suddenly feel that there's no such real I, no such emotional I, no I existing from its own side. There is I, because there are the aggregates, but the I is nothing other than what is merely imputed by the mind. That's all it is. There should be the same understanding, the same awareness, with all the rest, down to the particles of the atoms and the split-seconds of consciousness. That awareness should be the same with everything. Whether we are listening to a teaching, walking or doing something else, in reality there's no concrete, real I existing from its own side. All these things that appear to us and in which we believe are total hallucinations; they are all totally empty. Not even an atom of them exists.

While we are walking, we should practice mindfulness of this. "I am walking, but what is that I? Nothing except what is merely labeled by the mind. That I is doing the action of walking." It is the same with the aggregates. It is the same with everything, down to the particles of the atoms. We should practice mindfulness of this when we are walking, sitting or doing any other activity. There are piles of labels. Practice mindfulness that all these phenomena exist in mere name, being merely labeled by the mind.

When you meditate like this, the understanding that comes in your heart is that these things are all empty of the real one existing from its own side. You can see that while they all exist, they're empty. Starting with the I, everything unifies emptiness and dependent arising. This is what Guru Shakyamuni Buddha has realized and shown, what Nagarjuna has realized and shown, what Milarepa has realized and shown, what Lama Tsongkhapa has realized and shown.

If you practice mindfulness in this way, you don't allow your mind to create the concept of ignorance. If you let your mind hold on to the truly existent appearance, believing it to be true, you are then creating ignorance all the time. The antidote to that is to practice mindfulness all the time that everything exists in mere name, being merely labeled by the mind. If you are practicing mindfulness of this all the time, you don't allow your mind to create this ignorance that is the root of samsara. You don't create the self-grasping of the person and the self-grasping of the aggregates, or phenomena. By practicing mindfulness, you don't create this root of samsara.

Here in *The Bodhisattva's Jewel Garland* it says:

> With remembrance, awareness and conscientiousness,
> Always protect the doors of your senses.

We protect ourselves from delusion, particularly from ignorance. Another type of ignorance is ignorance of karma. Even though we might intellectually know about karma, in our daily life we sometimes don't recognize that we are creating negative karma. Sometimes we don't know that what we are doing is negative karma. That's ignorance of karma.

Before, I mentioned piles of labels, but even that is wrong because it is still gross. When you think of one label on top of another label, it still makes you think that a truly existent I, a real I, is on the aggregates. The I is labeled in dependence upon the aggregates; but if you think that the I is on the aggregates, it's easy to fall into thinking that there's something real there. Because there are the aggregates, the mind merely imputed the I, and that's how it is existing and functioning, as merely imputed by the mind. Even thinking of the piles of labels is still not quite correct, because it makes you believe there's some real I that can be found on the aggregates. The idea that the I can be found on the aggregates shouldn't be there *at all.* Otherwise, you can't differentiate the view of the Prasangika school from that of the Svatantrika school. The subtlest difference between these schools is that the Svatantrika school believes that the I exists by its nature and can be found on the aggregates. There's no such belief in the Prasangika school. The I not only doesn't truly exist, but it doesn't exist even by its nature. There's no such thing there— you cannot find the I on the aggregates. There are huge differences between these two Madhyamaka schools.

December 30

Though I don't remember whether I've received the commentary, I have received the oral transmission of *The Bodhisattva's Jewel Garland* by Lama Atisha. So, there is the lineage. Because it is quite short, I thought to go over Lama Atisha's advice as part of the Kadampa teachings.

> Abandon all doubts;
> Definitely cherish the practice.

What is the practice that we should definitely cherish? There's no practice other than the lam-rim. What we should understand here is that it means the lam-rim.

As Lama Tsongkhapa explains in the lam-rim prayer *The Foundation of All Good Qualities:*

Seeking samsaric pleasures is the door to all suffering:

They are uncertain and cannot be relied upon.

Recognizing these shortcomings,

Please bless me to generate the strong wish for the bliss of

    liberation.[18]

This is a very powerful meditation. I was actually going to quote the next verse,[19] but hearing this verse first helps us to see why Lama Tsongkhapa stressed living in morality as the essential practice. We can then see the purpose of doing this essential practice.

The verse says that no matter how much we use samsaric enjoyments, we never find satisfaction. We have had every samsaric enjoyment there is numberless times. We have had all the human beings' pleasures and all the devas' pleasures, which are a million times more pleasurable than the sense enjoyments of the wealthiest human being in the richest country. We have had all these enjoyments numberless times; we have had every enjoyment of human beings and devas numberless times during time without beginning.

NOTHING IS DEFINITE

As mentioned in the lam-rim teachings, in the section on the six shortcomings of samsara, nothing is definite. Nothing is definite in

---

[18] *Essential Buddhist Prayers: Volume 1*, p. 140.

[19] Led by this pure thought,
Mindfulness, alertness and great caution arise.
The root of the teachings is keeping the pratimoksha vows:
Please bless me to accomplish this essential practice.

Understanding the nature of samsara—the changes in relation-ships, with your meeting the same beings again and again but with different relationships—helps with the grief you feel when a family member has passed away. Otherwise, missing them so much, you can grieve for them for a long time, even for the rest of your life. Thinking of the nature of samsara can help: you have had all these different relationships with that person numberless times, and you will also have different relationships with them in the future. Some-times, when the husband dies and the wife is left alone or the wife dies and the husband is left alone, the husband or wife has been the only person that they depended on their whole life. If the husband, the only person she has depended on her whole life, passes away, the wife can't stand to be left alone with no one to depend on. The wife can't bear it, and because of her grief, many times she also soon dies. Or it can happen the other way around. As I mentioned, there is no need to worry as they'll meet that person again in future lives. Hearing that can help the person to feel better.

THE SHORTCOMINGS OF FOLLOWING DESIRE

This verse from *The Foundation of All Good Qualities* is saying that no matter how much we enjoy samsaric pleasures, we can never find satisfaction, and that it is the door to all suffering. By realizing the shortcomings of samsaric perfections, that there's nothing definite about them, we ask to be granted blessings to have great longing for the happiness of liberation, which is ultimate happiness.

No matter how much you enjoy samsaric happiness, you can

never find satisfaction. Take alcoholics, for example. They drink the first sip, then the second sip, then the third sip, then more and more, and then lose control. They can't stop. Because they are unable to get satisfaction, they drink more and more, then become totally uncontrolled. They then have no sense of shame, and all the secrets they have come out. If they talk about everybody's faults, it can cause a quarrel or a fight, with people even killing each other. When they're not drinking, they don't usually say anything; but when they drink they become uncontrolled, with no sense of shame or shyness. They then express everything, whether anger or something else, to other people. And because there's no control, many people also die unnecessarily in car accidents. They endanger not only themselves but the other people in their car, as well as people in other cars; not only do they die but also other people. At home, they cause a lot of problems to their husband or wife or other family members, with quarreling, breaking things and beatings. They put themselves through so many years of education, starting from kindergarten, then finally get a job, earn money and buy a house with every material comfort. They then destroy those things and cause a lot of unnecessary harm to their family and to themselves. Being alcoholic makes their own life so difficult. These are shortcomings of following desire.

Alcoholics live their whole life like this, until they totally destroy everything. They are even unable to do their jobs properly; it becomes an obstacle even to their jobs. They then lose their job, and there is the financial burden of that. Their family throws them out, and they become homeless. There are so many homeless people in London, New York and other big cities, many of them alcoholics.

Their family cannot take care of them, so they then become homeless. And they are still alcoholics. They spend even the little money
that they collect on drink.

Alcoholics totally destroy the precious human body that they
have received just once, this time. They make it totally meaningless.
When Khunu Lama, Tenzin Gyaltsen, gave a commentary to *Lamp
of the Path to Enlightenment* in Nepal, Rinpoche talked to the audience
about the shortcomings of drinking alcohol. Rinpoche said, "You
fall down in the road in your own vomit. Dogs then come and lick
up what you have vomited, right to your mouth." I remember Rinpoche talking about that.

I've been talking just about the mistakes of following desire for
alcohol, but the shortcomings of following desire for drugs are similar. You get more and more addicted to the drugs, then it becomes
unbelievably difficult to control because you crave that pleasure so
much. Because of that, you then steal from shops or from your parents, and you engage in various other negative karmas. Following
desire, grasping the pleasure of taking drugs, leads to your becoming more and more addicted, which makes your life more and more
difficult. It then leads to your lying, stealing, killing and committing
many other negative karmas. Again, your precious human body,
which is received this one time, is totally destroyed; it becomes
totally meaningless. You end up in prison again and again. You
come out of prison, do the same thing again because you can't control your desire, then again end up in prison.

In relation to business, there are also shortcomings of following
desire. No matter how much profit you're able to make, because you

don't control your desire, you want more and more. If you make a profit of $1,000, you want $10,000. If you are then able to make $10,000, you want $100,000. If you make $100,000, you want to make a million dollars. If you are able to make a million dollars, you then want a billion dollars. If you are able to make a billion dollars, you then want to make a trillion dollars. And if you make a trillion dollars, you then want to make a zillion dollars. It goes on and on, without end. If you follow desire, there's no end. No matter how much money you get, you want more and more. In business, the mistakes of following desire have no end.

You then have so much worry and fear about others becoming wealthier than you or about losing what you have. Before you were wealthy, you didn't have those problems. With wealth, you have new problems that you didn't have before. When you start to be wealthy, the problems of having wealth start.) ⅹ

Because you are continuously following desire, after some time you don't have the karma, the merit, to continue to be successful. You have already used up the merit you collected in the past to be successful; that merit is finished. One day your whole business suddenly collapses, and you lose millions or billions of dollars. You don't normally have to worry about how to pay for your food, rent and other family expenses, but suddenly you are greatly concerned about how you will even be able to take care of your family.

If you had stopped following desire and been content, if you had stopped expanding your business before it collapsed, there would have been no problem. But because you followed desire and continued to expand, one day you lost everything, even what you had ing the previous years. Or because you are following

ıting more and more, after some time you engage in ille-

es. Even though it mightn't be known about in the begin-

ning, after some years your business partner or somebody else who

gets upset with you will expose the illegal things you have done.

Then, after all this, you end up in prison or with a very bad reputa-

tion. The whole country is talking about what you have done, and

you can't do anything about it. These are some of the shortcomings

of following desire in relation to business. In recent years on TV you

have seen this happen many times to wealthy people. Somebody

sues them, and they end up like this.

There are also shortcomings of following desire in connection

to relationships, where you're not satisfied with what you have

and always want something better. In this field, there is unbeliev-

able suffering, and the suffering is increasing all the time. Because

of following desire and not being content, you have relationships

with many people, which then creates hell in your family. Your own

life and the life of your partner become hell. You are not yet born

in hell, but it's as if you're in hell. There are then court cases, and

along with that, so much worry and fear and hundreds of problems,

including unnecessary expense. When the husband or wife finds

out about their partner, it becomes a double prison, a double hell.

It is then very easy for the thought of suicide to come; it is very easy

to think of killing yourself or of killing others. Again, your desire

causes you to engage in various negative karmas: lying, insulting,

speaking harshly, slandering in order to cause a separation, steal-

ing, killing. It opens the door to so many negative karmas in this life. It is like you are sunk in a quagmire, drowning in mud. You are suffocating. And it goes on and on in this way. The pain is in your heart and the other person's heart for years, as well as in the hearts of many other people. For years and years there is so much pain in your heart; it doesn't heal easily.

Being unable to do pure Dharma practice is also one of the shortcomings of desire. Because you are attached to reputation, power or receiving offerings, you are unable to do pure Dharma practice. Desire for all those things becomes an obstacle to your practice, to being able to continuously practice pure Dharma and have realizations. Another shortcoming of following desire is that even if you have taken vows of ordination, as you don't practice contentment but continuously follow desire, you will degenerate your vows more and more. You will be unable to live purely in your vows. It will become more and more difficult for you to live in your vows, and then you will even break a root vow. Following desire brings greater and greater harm to your vows.

When you follow desire, because your mind is so distracted by the object of attachment, if you are doing a meditation session or a retreat, you will be unable to concentrate even during the recitation of one mala of OM MANI PADME HUM. Even though you try to make time to practice Dharma, to recite mantras or to do retreat or meditation sessions, because you are following desire, the eight worldly dharmas arise and don't allow your mind to focus well on the object of concentration, even though you know that life is short and death can happen at any time.

You can meditate on the shortcomings of desire in these different ways. From these examples you can see that enjoying samsaric happiness doesn't bring satisfaction, and it becomes the door to all suffering.

In the following lines of the verse from *The Foundation of All Good Qualities*, you request to be granted blessings to be able to realize the shortcomings of samsaric perfections, which are uncertain, and to then give rise to a great longing for the happiness of liberation. The indefinite nature of the perfections of samsara includes having to leave whatever beautiful body you have taken in samsara. Everything has to be left. And you have to join again and again to the next samsara. Even if you become high, even if you are born in the tip of samsara, the highest level of the formless realm—there are limitless sky, limitless consciousness, nothingness and then the tip of samsara—you again fall down, even into the hell realms. As mentioned in the teachings, even if you have a body full of light like that of a Deva's Son, after that you can be reborn in an animal realm where you don't see any light your whole life. After you become high, you then become low. And, as I mentioned before, meeting ends with separation and birth ends with death. And after collection, there is exhaustion. All these shortcomings of samsara are contained in this verse.

THE HEART PRACTICE

The next verse of *The Foundation of All Good Qualities* says:

> Led by this pure thought,
> Mindfulness, alertness and great caution arise.

The root of the teachings is keeping the pratimoksha vows:
Please bless me to accomplish this essential practice.

Led by this pure thought means realizing how samsara is only in the nature of suffering by having meditated as I have just explained. By realizing how samsara and even samsaric perfections are only in the nature of suffering, you have no attachment to samsara and samsaric perfections, and you generate the thought of seeking liberation. It's a pure thought, unstained by attachment, and practice of the pratimoksha vows is inspired by that pure thought. Living in the pratimoksha vows on the basis of remembrance and awareness of renunciation of samsara is the heart practice, the essential practice. You ask for blessings to be able to live in the pratimoksha vows as the essential practice.

Another way of saying this is that you must cherish living in the pratimoksha vows as your heart practice. Lay people living in lay vows cherish that as their heart practice, and of course, those who are ordained do the same thing. Other traditions talk about doing large numbers of prostrations, Vajrasattva mantras and other preliminary practices, but in the Lama Tsongkhapa tradition, as explained in the lam-rim teachings by Pabongka Dechen Nyingpo, the main practice is not the preliminaries but the pratimoksha vows. If we cherish our pratimoksha vows as the essential practice, we don't create much negative karma, so we then don't need to do many preliminary practices. The meaning behind this is that we don't need to do so many preliminary practices because our life is pure.

ABANDONING DOUBTS

Here I want to talk further on the advice to abandon all doubts, which I explained yesterday. When you haven't learnt much about Dharma, it looks as if you have no doubts, but then as you learn more and more, you have more and more doubts. The more you learn, the more questions you have. However, along with the learning, you practice and experience the path; you collect merit and purify your negative karmas and defilements, which are what hinder your clear understanding and cause you to have doubts. When you do the practice of purification at the same time as you are learning, experiences and realizations of the path then come. When you achieve the arya, or exalted, paths—the path of seeing and the path of meditation—you are able to directly perceive emptiness, which actually ceases the defilements, the disturbing-thought obscurations. Especially, by achieving the Mahayana path of seeing and the Mahayana path of meditation, you cease the disturbing-thought obscurations you haven't ceased before by proceeding along the Hinayana path. However, with the Mahayana path of seeing and path of meditation, you also cease the subtle defilements.

Here I would like to say that when you complete the path to enlightenment, having ceased all the gross and subtle defilements and completed all understanding, at that time you don't have a single doubt. When your mind becomes fully awakened, there's not one single doubt. You have then removed even the four causes of unknowing, which arhats and even tenth bhumi bodhisattvas haven't removed.[21] You have no doubts even in regard to subtle karmas.

The ultimate cutting of doubts comes through your experience, through actualizing the path more and more. That's the real way to cut doubts.

HOW TO BE HAPPY TO PRACTICE DHARMA

The next verse in *The Bodhisattva's Jewel Garland* is:

> Thoroughly abandon sleep, drowsiness and laziness.
> Always attempt to have perseverance.

Perseverance is a mind that is happy to practice Dharma. The easiest, most powerful way to have perseverance is by reflecting on impermanence and death. First reflect on how precious this human body with eight freedoms and ten richnesses is, how you can achieve the three great meanings with it, how it will be difficult to find such a body again and how you will have it just this one time. On the basis of this, remember that death can happen at any time. Impermanence and death is very powerful—the most powerful meditation for us beginners. Also, relate impermanence and death to negative karma and its result, rebirth in the lower realms. Remember again

---

[21] Mi she gyi zhi: not knowing karmic causes due to the separation of (1) time or (2) space or to (3) their subtlety, and not knowing an enlightened being's secret qualities and actions.

and again the unimaginable sufferings of the hell beings, hungry ghosts and animals. As Nagarjuna explains, we should remember the hot and cold hells every day. Nagarjuna advises this because when we think of the hot and cold hells we have no space in our mind for attachment and anger, these negative emotional thoughts that disturb and obscure our mind.

Whenever thoughts of the happiness of this life comes, we delay or stop our practice. Whenever attachment clinging to this life comes, laziness comes, and we don't want to practice. We want to spend our time enjoying the comforts of this life instead of practicing Dharma. At that time we should remember that death can happen at any time. Then what happens after that? The most unbearable suffering. We can't bear even a small problem in this human realm; we can't bear to have a headache, a toothache, some stomach pain or even to be a little hot or a little cold. When we experience even a small problem in this human realm, because we can't bear it, we give up practicing Dharma.

Think, "If I were now in the lower realms, in the hot or cold hells, in the preta realm or in the animal realm, my suffering would be far greater. The hunger and thirst of the preta realm is thousands of times greater that that of the human realm. Leaving aside the major hot and cold hells, if I were born now in a neighboring hell or even an ordinary hell realm, my suffering would be unbelievable."

We can't bear to put our finger in boiling hot water; but compared to being born in the neighboring hell where there are oceans of lava, the boiling hot water of the human realm is extremely cold. Imagine suddenly being in such a hell.

Death can happen any day, any hour, any moment—even this moment. And what comes after death is the lower realms. As Nagarjuna advises, we should remember the unbearable sufferings of the lower realms.

The cause of rebirth in the lower realms is negative karma, or nonvirtuous action, and any activity we do with a motivation of attachment clinging to this life is a nonvirtue. For example, if we got dressed today with a motivation of attachment clinging to this life, that action of dressing became nonvirtuous because our motivation was nonvirtuous. What was our motivation when we were washing? For many of us, it was simply attachment clinging to the happiness and comfort of this life, so again that washing became negative karma. It was the same when we ate lunch and dinner, and it will be the same when we go to sleep. With any activity we do, if we analyze our motivation for doing it, we find it is nonvirtuous, attachment clinging to this life, so all those activities become negative karma.

Negative karma is very extensive. It's not limited to just the ten nonvirtuous actions, but within the ten nonvirtuous actions are those nonvirtues that we collect many times every day—though we mightn't kill or steal. However His Holiness Ling Rinpoche once made the comment that the subject of stealing is extensive and detailed. It depends on the individual person, but we generally commit many of the ten nonvirtues many times in one day. We also break the vows we have taken: pratimoksha vows, lay or ordained; bodhisattva vows; tantric vows. This is talking about just today. The negative karmas we have created from the time of our birth in this life are unimaginable, and then there are all the negative karmas we have created in beginningless past lives.

In his lam-rim teachings, Pabongka Dechen Nyingpo says that an ordained person being careless about and not immediately confessing a downfall is heavier negative karma than having killed one hundred human beings and one hundred horses. (I don't think it has to be only horses—it can be any animal. In the past in Tibet they used horses a lot as there were no cars.) If you have taken ordination and are intentionally careless about your vows, this is how heavy the karma that you create is.

When you think of how death can happen at any time and of the lower realms, in relation to karma, you can't ignore it. You have to get up and practice. You can't stand it. You've got to do something immediately; you've got to purify, collect merit, meditate on the path.

It is also very useful to think about people you know who have died, like Andrea [Antonietti], the Italian monk. On my advice, he took ordination for a second time and died as a monk. Many of us here, those who have been here in Bodhgaya and in Dharamsala many times, will remember Andrea. He was an old student, an Italian, who was a monk before. He then changed his life, but before he died, while he was sick, he again took ordination. Now he's gone. He doesn't exist. There's no Andrea. Before there was Andrea, but now there's not. Before we used to joke and play with him and enjoy his humble, good personality, but now he doesn't exist. Think, "It is the same with me. There will come a time when I don't exist any more, a time when I'm not here in this world. This could happen at any time. By this time next year, I could be the same as Andrea, whom we can't see, who doesn't exist in this world. This could happen. By this time next year, I could be like that—not to be seen in this world. Some people have Andrea's malas and other possessions; the same thing could happen to me. Any day this could happen to me."

There was also another Italian, Stefano [Piovella]. He was a monk before, but he wasn't a monk when he died. It is the same. We used to joke and play with him, making fun of him all the time, but now he's not here. Now he's not here in this world. Think, "Exactly the same thing could happen to me at any time. I could be gone from this world. I won't exist. This could happen at any time."

There was also Tenzin Konchog, the nun who was here making tsa-tsas about five years ago. She was the main person responsible for making tsa-tsas. A few years ago she was here, in Bodhgaya, but now she is not here. She's gone. Think, "Exactly the same thing could happen to me any time, any day. I will not be here. There's a time when I will be gone from this world. I won't exist. This could happen any day."

Your body could be carried to the cemetery or the crematorium. Any day this could happen. You could suddenly have a heart attack or a stroke. Something could suddenly happen, and the time of your death come. Your precious human life would be gone.

If you had done continual strong practice of purification, practiced morality well, lived your life with bodhicitta and correctly devoted yourself to the virtuous friend, you would have no regrets. Even if some sickness came and your death happened, it wouldn't disturb you. It wouldn't upset you at all. You would be very happy, as you would feel completely confident that you would go to a pure land or receive a perfect human body in your next life. Your mind would be happy, or at least you would have no fear. Even if death suddenly came to you, you would not be frightened of being born in the lower realms.

If we really bring our attention inside, if we really think about the nature of our life, impermanence and death, we realize that our death could happen at any time and, in particular, all the unimaginable sufferings of the lower realms could happen at any time. Relate this to all the negative karmas you do—in one day there are so many, like rainfall. Committing one complete nonvirtuous action has four suffering results. One of them is creating the result similar to the cause, which means doing that action again, which again produces four suffering results, one of which is creating the result similar to the cause, so you commit the action again…. It goes on and on in this way. Committing one complete nonvirtuous action, from the ten nonvirtuous actions, produces suffering results that go on and on and on, so that there is unending suffering of samsara.

We've done so many of the ten nonvirtuous actions in this life, since our birth, and so many others during beginningless rebirths. The results of them will go on and on in that way. There are numberless of them left on our mental continuum that we haven't purified and that we haven't finished experiencing.

Since committing even one negative karma from the ten brings this endless ongoing suffering, you can't stand it. You have to get rid of it, purify it, immediately. It's as if you have swallowed some poison and could die at any time. It's as if a poisonous snake has bitten you: the poison is spreading and you could die at any time. But ingesting poison or being bitten by a poisonous snake is nothing. That alone can't make you be reborn in the lower realms, but your negative karma can.

I've been talking about just one negative karma, but we have created so many negative karmas today, in this life and during beginningless past lives. There's no way you can stand it—you have to purify it all right away! And at this time, by having received this perfect human body, you have all the opportunities to purify it. If death comes before you have purified your negative karma, you are finished. When will you meet Dharma again? When will you be able to purify all those negative karmas? When will you be able to actualize the path? It is extremely difficult to say.

Now, on top of having committed the ten nonvirtuous actions and degenerated or broken all three levels of vows, you have collected negative karma in relation to the guru. Even the smallest of these negative karmas is very powerful, and you have created so many with heresy, anger and other negative thoughts. These negative karmas are much heavier than all those others.

In the lam-rim outline of the shortcomings of having made mistakes in correctly devoting to the guru, the first shortcoming is that criticizing the guru is like criticizing all the buddhas.

Second, if you get angry with your guru, you destroy eons of merit equal in number to the moments of your anger, and for the same number of eons you will be reborn in hell and experience suffering.

Third, even though you practice tantra, you won't achieve the sublime realization.

Fourth, even though you attempt to practice tantra, it will be like achieving hell. Even though you practice tantra for many years by not sleeping, not eating, not talking and living alone in a cave, it will be like achieving hell. Why? Here you have to understand that when you make a mistake in devoting to the virtuous friend—even showing some small disrespect, criticizing him, harming him or giving rise to negative thoughts—it is so heavy that even though you are practicing virtue and collecting merit by doing retreat sessions, it is very small compared to the heavy negative karma you have collected in relation to the virtuous friend. That negative karma is so huge that any virtue you practice by reciting mantras and so forth becomes insignificant. The negative karma is overwhelming, and you are reborn in the hell realm. This is what happens unless you change your mind, stop following those negative thoughts, recognize the mistakes you have made, confess them to the guru and purify them. By using logical reasoning and the quotations from Shakyamuni Buddha and Vajradhara, you have to transform your mind into devotion by seeing the guru as a buddha.

It doesn't mean that you have no hope—it's not saying that. There's hope, if you change, if you recognize the mistakes you have made and, with strong regret, confess and purify them. In order not to commit the mistakes again, you then have to keep your mind in devotion toward that guru. You can change; it's not saying you can't change. But if you don't change, no matter what practice you do—many years of chanting mantras in retreat with no food and no sleep—even though you may be collecting merit, it will be insignificant compared to the heaviness of the negative karma you have created. *Even though you attempt to practice tantra, it will be like achieving hell.* As long as you don't change, it will be like achieving hell. Instead of achieving enlightenment, you'll be achieving hell, because that karma is so heavy.

What I am saying is that there's no time to be lazy. Reflect on the negative karmas you have collected and the sufferings of the lower realms, and remember that this is the only chance you have. If you cherish yourself, if you love yourself, this is what you have to do. If you want to take care of yourself, this is the practice you need to do. If you think about this, there's no time for laziness, no time to be distracted by the appearances of this life or works for this life.

As mentioned in the motivation for taking the Eight Mahayana Precepts by my root guru, His Holiness Trijang Rinpoche,[22] which is similar to the motivation for taking refuge in *Jorchö*, if you think of all the endless sufferings of samsara that you will have to experience, particularly those of the lower realms, you don't dare to eat or sleep. When you're very frightened, you can't eat, or even if you do manage to eat, you vomit. If you think of all the past beginningless sufferings of samsara, in particular those of the three lower realms, it's something that cracks your heart. It's very frightening.

Here *The Bodhisattva's Jewel Garland* says:

Thoroughly abandon sleep, drowsiness and laziness.
Always attempt to have perseverance.

---

[22] See Lama Zopa Rinpoche's *The Direct and Unmistaken Method* at LamaYeshe.com.

Of course, it's not saying not to sleep at all at night. There is sleeping yoga. I heard that His Holiness Chogye Trichen Rinpoche sleeps for only two or three hours, and sometimes only one hour. During the daytime he gives initiations and teachings, then does his own practice for many hours. Also, I think His Holiness the Dalai Lama gets up around three o'clock in the morning. Peljor-la, His Holiness's attendant, offers tea around 3:30, then His Holiness begins his practice. Of course, Compassion Buddha doesn't need to practice....

As mentioned in *The Great Treatise on the Stages of the Path to Enlightenment*, in the middle part of the night you do sleeping yoga, then you wake up very early in the morning and practice. My sleeping is at the wrong time, the totally wrong time. When it's time to practice, I'm sleeping.

> With remembrance, awareness and conscientiousness,
> Always protect the doors of your senses.
> Three times day and night, again and again,
> Examine your mental continuum.

You have to protect your body, speech and mind from engaging in negative actions. As mentioned, three times in the daytime and three times at night, you should examine your mental continuum.

ABANDONING ATTACHMENT

What makes you attached to an object comes from your own mind, not from the side of the object. One point is that an imprint has been left on your mind in the past, and the imprint projects that view, or appearance, of an object as attractive. It's projected by the imprint left on your mental continuum from your past concept of attachment, your past habituation. That is why you see an object—someone's body, for example—as something good, or beautiful, and are attached to the pleasure of having contact with it. This view of the object came from your mind; it is projected by the imprint. There's no such beautiful thing there, appearing from the side of the object. Your past imprint projected this view, and your mind interpreted, "This is nice, something worth being attached to." From the male side, there is a projection on a female body; from the female side, on a male body. It's just a physical body, but the past imprint left on the mind interprets that it's good. After this projection and this interpretation, attachment then arises and clings to that body.

There's really nothing there but the view, the creation, of your own mind. Your own mind made it up. As I normally explain, two factors are involved in how something comes from your own mind. One is your present concept: your view is a creation of your present concept. The other factor is long-term: it is the view of your past karma.

For example, you may have been seeing someone's body for a long time, for many years, but no attachment to it has ever arisen. Then suddenly one day your view of that person's body changes. You exaggerate its good qualities, thinking that it is wonderful or beautiful. Attachment then arises to that object you have exaggerated, and you cling to it.

One point is that your view of that body as beautiful comes from your present concept. It's a creation of your concept of today, of this moment. It's exactly like a movie being projected onto a screen from a film in a projector. Attachment then clings to that projection.

The other point is the past karmic imprint. Seeing this person in this way happens because of past karma. There has been a connection, a relationship, in the past with that being. Even though the person might be ugly in the view of many other people, you see them as beautiful. Of course, it has to do with your present concept, but there's also a long-term evolution, which has to do with your past karma. Your past karma produced, or projected, your view of the person as beautiful, even though in the view of other people they are ugly.

You can see here that nothing exists from the object's side. It comes purely from your own mind. Everything comes just from your own mind, from your present concept and your past karma. This is one very important analysis you can do when you encounter an object of anger or attachment. There's really no such thing there. You have this view because of your own past karmic imprint, but since you're not aware of this, you believe it exists totally from its own side, from the object's side. You then think it's worth being attached to that object, attachment arises, and you cling to that object.

To show how there's nothing from the side of the object, I normally use the example of learning the alphabet. When you were a child, your teacher or parents taught you the alphabet. At that time, when your teacher first drew the lines for the letter A on the blackboard, you just saw the lines. Before you were taught, "This is A," you just saw the lines. At that time you didn't see those lines as A; there was no appearance of A to you. Why didn't you have any appearance of these lines as A? Because your mind hadn't yet labeled them "A." Why not? Because nobody had yet introduced them to you as A. That's why you saw just lines and had no view of them as A.

Your teacher then told you, "This is A." By listening to and believing their explanation, you then labeled those lines "A." Your mind then merely imputed "A" to those lines and believed in that label your mind had imputed. As a result A then appeared to you. After that you saw those lines as A. For you to be able to see that figure as A, all this evolution had to take place. I've used the example of A here and not that of a body, but we should analyze and meditate in the same way with any body that is an object of our attachment. And it is the same with any object of anger. Here, you can see that this view of A, this appearance of A, came from your mind. It's a creation of your mind. Your mind labeled "A" by following and believing in what somebody taught you.

You can now see that A is labeled. The A that you see is labeled by your mind; it came from your mind. It's very clear. At the very beginning, when you hadn't been introduced to the alphabet, you didn't see that figure as A; it didn't appear to you as A because your mind hadn't yet labeled, "This is A." It is the same with all phenomena, including all the objects of the eye-sense, all the forms and colors you see here. Everything that you can see here came from your mind, through labeling. What you see, what appears to you, is what your mind has merely imputed.

It is the same with sounds. Any sound that you hear is what your mind has merely imputed. What your ear-sense hears is the base, and in relation to that base, your mind then makes up the label "sound." So, "sound" is the label that is merely imputed to the base, the phenomenon that the ear-sense hears. Depending upon the quality of the base, whether it's a song being sung, a prayer being chanted or music being played, you then label, or merely impute, "good singing" or "bad singing," "good chanting" or "bad chanting," "good music" or "bad music." Here you can see the difference between the label "sound" and the base of the sound.

It is also the same with the objects of your tongue-sense. You are tasting what your mind has merely imputed. The taste that is appearing to you is what your mind has merely imputed. And what is appearing to the body-sense—soft, rough, good, bad—is what is merely imputed by the mind.

It is the same with all five external sense objects that you experience. What you see, what you hear, what you smell, what you taste, what you touch—they are all what your mind has merely imputed. Therefore, they all came from your own mind; they are all creations of your own mind. You are seeing, hearing, smelling, tasting and touching what your mind has merely imputed.

Through this analysis you can now understand that with any object of attachment, whether someone's body or something else, you're seeing nothing there that your mind hasn't labeled, that your mind hasn't merely imputed; you are seeing nothing that doesn't come from your mind, that doesn't depend on your mind. In the same way, any object of anger or of ignorance also comes from your mind.

However, even though all phenomena exist in mere name, being merely imputed by mind, they appear to us to be not merely labeled by mind. This view came from ignorance; it is a creation of ignorance. The imprint left on our mental continuum projected, or decorated, true existence on the merely labeled phenomena. This negative imprint projected all these hallucinations of true existence onto the merely labeled phenomena, which are empty of existing from their own side. It projected a truly existent appearance all over the merely labeled I, merely labeled mind, merely labeled body, merely labeled hell, merely labeled enlightenment, merely labeled four noble truths, merely labeled everything. The view of ignorance came from our mind, from the negative imprint, and that is the basis of anger and attachment. All these hallucinations have covered the reality of I, action, object, and all other phenomena, which exist in mere name, merely imputed by mind. Past ignorance left the negative imprint on the mental continuum, which then projected all these hallucinations. It made everything appear real, existent from its own side, and not merely labeled by mind.

Now here, in the view of ignorance, you have someone's real body, in the sense of existing from its own side, not merely labeled by mind. You exaggerate that body as being beautiful, then right after that, attachment arises. (Or you exaggerate something as being bad, then right after that, anger arises.) You exaggerate that object as being beautiful, attachment then arises, and you cling to that object. So, there's another hallucination. On top of that fundamental hallucination of true existence, you exaggerate that object as beautiful, and attachment then arises and clings to that object. Or, on top of the fundamental hallucination of a truly existent appearance, you exaggerate an object's bad qualities, then anger arises toward that object. So, there's a double hallucination. In reality there's no such thing there.

With the object of anger, or ill will, you want to hurt that object. With the object of attachment, you cling to it, and it becomes difficult for you to separate from the object, just as it's difficult to separate oil from paper or cloth or difficult to separate a moth from candle wax. In reality, all this came from your own mind. There's no such object of anger or attachment there. It is something you have built up on top of the view of ignorance, the truly existent appearance. The foundation is a total hallucination. There's no such thing there. There's no such truly existent body, no such real body in the sense of existing from its own side. It's totally empty—not even an atom of that exists. All these objects are the view of a hallucinated mind.

Therefore, giving rise to attachment or anger is total nonsense. When you think of how the object of attachment or anger has been created by your own mind, attachment and anger don't arise. These negative emotional thoughts arise only when you think that there is such a real good or bad thing, one existing from its own side.

As Lama Tsongkhapa explains, in reference to a quotation from *Four Hundred Stanzas* by Aryadeva, on the nature that is exaggerated by this ignorance, we then exaggerate especially beauty and ugliness. After that, attachment, anger and other delusions arise. The way the delusions apprehend objects can be eliminated by valid reasoning.

While you are in equipoise meditation on emptiness, seeing everything as empty, ignorance, because it is the opposite of wisdom, cannot at the same time project a truly existent appearance. In that way you can also stop anger, which apprehends an object as bad and wishes to harm it, and attachment, which clings to objects.

Lama Tsongkhapa also quotes an explanation from a commentary to *Four Hundred Stanzas*, which says that attachment and so forth only exaggerate as beautiful or ugly phenomena that have been labeled by ignorance. Because of that, attachment is not separate from ignorance; it is dependent on ignorance. Ignorance is the principal delusion.

The conclusion is that attachment and anger are total nonsense. There's no need to give rise to attachment or anger in relation to objects. This is one very deep meditation to protect the doors of the senses, to protect your mind from delusion. Not only that, but with this way of meditating by recognizing the object of refutation, the truly existent phenomenon, and thinking that it is a hallucination exaggerated by ignorance, there is then no basis for any delusion to arise. Simply thinking that the fundamental hallucination is a hallucination is like dropping an atomic bomb on all the delusions.

December 31

Think, "No matter how long it takes or how difficult it is, I must achieve full enlightenment in order to free the sentient beings, who have been my mother and kind numberless times during beginningless rebirths, from the oceans of samsaric suffering and lead them to full enlightenment by myself alone. To do that, I first need to actualize the graduated path to enlightenment. Therefore, I'm going to listen to the holy Dharma, to *The Bodhisattva's Jewel Garland* by Lama Atisha, the originator of the Kadampa tradition."

How to be happy to practice Dharma

I just want to mention a little more on the verse I discussed yesterday:

Abandon sleep, drowsiness and laziness.
Always attempt to have perseverance.

Last night I mentioned how important it is, especially for us beginners, to remember impermanence and death. As mentioned in the benefits of remembering impermanence and death, by remembering impermanence and death we are able to overcome delusions, which is very difficult to do because we are habituated to them. We have been under the control of delusions during beginningless time, during beginningless samsaric lifetimes. However, by remembering impermanence and death, we are able to overcome delusions and destroy them. Also, by remembering impermanence and death, we are able to begin to practice Dharma, to generate the path. We are also able to continue our Dharma practice, to continue actualizing the path. Also, by remembering impermanence and death, we are able to complete our Dharma practice, to complete the path, and achieve enlightenment.

Remembering impermanence and death is very important when we begin our Dharma practice; it's also very important to remember it in the middle; and it's very important to remember it even at the end. When our death comes, we can then die very happily. We won't have any fears about reincarnating in the lower realms and, on top of that, we will have an extremely joyful mind.

It's very helpful to write out quotations to remind you to bring your mind back into Dharma when it becomes distracted. It helps to write verses from *A Guide to the Bodhisattva's Way of Life* and other books on cards and put them around your room. It's like these teachings are saying, "Hey! Don't get distracted!" and then explaining the reasons why you shouldn't. For example, there is a quotation from Kharak Gomchung, one of the Kadampa geshes, which is similar to a verse in *A Guide to the Bodhisattva's Way of Life.*[23]

By depending on the human boat,
You cross the great river of suffering.
Since this boat will be difficult to find again,
While you have it, don't be lazy.

Write this verse out nicely on a beautiful card and put it up in your room as a reminder. When you then see these words, you'll know that you've immediately got to do something. You have to bring your attention back from the objects of delusion, from being distracted by the appearances of this life. You have to let go of your

[23] Ch. 7, v. 14.

grasping and clinging to these appearances and bring your mind into renunciation of this life, bodhicitta, right view or guru devotion. With those attitudes, you purify your mind, your negative karma and defilements; collect merit; and meditate on the path.

Also, *A Guide to the Bodhisattva's Way of Life* says:

> It's not certain which will come first—tomorrow or the next life. Therefore, rather than working for tomorrow, it's better to work for the next life.

This means it's better to try for long-term happiness, the happiness of all the coming future lives.

Kharak Gomchung also mentions:

> At present we have a choice between the happiness of the upper realms and the sufferings of the evil-gone realms. Reflect on this.

Also, in *Calling the Guru from Afar* Pabongka Dechen Nyingpo, the great enlightened being, the actual Heruka, describes how in each second we have the freedom to choose between the sufferings of the lower realms and the happiness of the upper realms, the human or deva realms.[24] It means we have the freedom to stop rebirth in

---

[24] "Thinking of this excellent body, highly meaningful and difficult to obtain, and wishing to take its essence with unerring choice between gain and loss, happiness and suffering—reminds me of you, Lama." See *Heart of the Path*, p. 403.

the lower realms and to receive the body of a happy transmigratory being. *Calling the Guru from Afar* says that when we reflect on this, it reminds us of the guru. That means the guru is the one who gives us this incredible opportunity, this freedom in each second to choose not to be reborn in the lower realms and to achieve at least the happiness of the upper realms. That is not our only choice. In every second we can also choose to create the cause to achieve liberation from samsara. Not only that, but in every second we have the incredible freedom to create the cause to achieve enlightenment.

When you see what is written in this verse, you then understand how each moment is unbelievably precious because you have the incredible freedom to accomplish all this. Of course, the only way to do this is to practice Dharma without even a second's delay. There's no way to achieve all this happiness without practicing Dharma.

To remind you of impermanence and death it's also helpful to have the belongings of somebody who has passed away. Every time you see or use those things it will remind you of impermanence and death. As I mentioned last night, you should think, "Like this person, I could no longer exist in this world, but have gone from here to my next life. This year, this month, this week, even today, even within this hour, I could be like this."

You did Medicine Buddha puja this morning for Peter [van Heeswijk], a big man from Holland, who went into a coma yesterday and suddenly died this morning. I also did a short prayer for him during my preparation for the Gyalwa Gyatso initiation.

Medicine Buddha puja or practice is always good to do for any problem but it is especially good to do at this most critical time of death. Medicine Buddha puja is one of the best things you can do to help someone who has died. In the past, during his time as a bodhisattva, Medicine Buddha did many prayers for us sentient beings, praying for us to have various problems pacified and to receive various good things. Medicine Buddha made many prayers that anyone who recited his name or mantra would be freed from these problems and have all this peace and happiness. After having achieved enlightenment, a buddha has many qualities, including the ten powers, one of which is the power of prayer. Once the power of prayer is achieved, the name and mantra of a buddha has the power to accomplish what was intended during that buddha's time as a bodhisattva. In this way, a buddha is able to benefit all sentient beings, immediately freeing them from suffering and bringing them happiness.

It is similar with the names of the Thirty-five Buddhas. If we recite one name just one time, we purify many eons of negative karma. In the past when the Thirty-five Buddhas generated bodhicitta and became bodhisattvas, they motivated in particular to benefit sentient beings by enabling them to purify negative karma. They motivated for their names to have the power to purify many eons of sentient beings' negative karma. They then attained enlightenment and achieved the power of prayer. This is why their names have so much power. By reciting one name one time, we can purify many eons of negative karma. For example, reciting Guru Shakyamuni Buddha's name one time has the power to purify 80,000 eons of negative karma, and some texts mention an even larger number. Lama Atisha explained that this is why reciting the Thirty-five Buddhas' names has so much power.

If you recite once the name of Tathagata Glorious Flower—*de zhin sheg pa me tog päl*, in Tibetan—it has the power to purify 100,000 eons of negative karma. And if you recite the mantra of this Tathagata—OM PUSHPA PUSHPA PUSHPA SVAHA—twenty-one times and offer a flower to a stupa, it helps to bring success.

Every time I went to Holland, Peter would come to see me, though I don't know whether he has been here in Bodhgaya during recent years. The last time I saw him was recently in France, when he came to a course. I did have a meeting with him, though I don't remember the topic of discussion. So, that's now the last time I will see him.

Peter, that student from Holland, has left this world. He has already gone. He suddenly went into a coma yesterday, then died. So, that could happen to you. Somehow you have been fortunate, and it hasn't happened so far. What happened to Peter could have happened to you a long time ago; you could have already died a long time ago. And if it had happened a long time ago or even last year, it's not sure where your consciousness would be by now. It's hard to say where you would be now.

By now you could have been born as a snake, constantly eating mice and other small animals. Because of negative karma, a snake has no other food. It can't eat vegetables or leaves. Their karma is to have to kill other sentient beings to survive.

Or you could have been born as a worm, living in filth and attacked by ants. Even if you were completely covered by ants, no matter how much pain you had, there would be nothing you could do. Think how painful it is when a single ant bites you on the leg.

Now think of this fragile worm completely covered by ants and being bitten all over its body. It can't do anything. So, you could have been like that by now.

Or you could have been born as a worm and already be in a bird's beak, with a little of your body hanging out and the rest inside. Your body could already have been chopped by a sharp beak. There would be nothing you could do except suffer. You could have been like that.

On TV I saw a program about a white worm that lives inside trees—it might have been somewhere in Africa. There's a hole in the trunk of a tree where the branches start, and this white worm lives some distance inside the wood. The karma is incredible. The worm is the food of a particular bird. The bird's beak isn't long, like a humming bird's, which is long enough to fit into flowers. Here the bird's beak isn't long enough to reach the worm, because it's quite a way down. However, tiny sticks, like tooth-picks only longer, grow from the tree. With its beak the bird breaks off one of these sticks and puts it down the hole. The bird doesn't get the worm immediately, because the worm's head has thick, brown skin. If the stick hits the head, it doesn't pierce the worm. It takes a little time. After two or three tries, however, the stick goes through the worm's body, probably because the worm moves around. The bird then takes out the stick with the worm on it and flies away.

It's amazing karma. The length of the stick is such that it exactly fits down the hole, and it also grows just there, on the same tree. The bird breaks the stick and puts it through the worm with its beak. By now you could have been like that—today, this hour, you could be like that.

Or you could have been born as a tiger. If tigers were vegetarian, they would be beautiful animals; but because of the manner in which they grab and eat other animals, they're terrifying. When a herd of buffaloes or some other animal races away, the calves and weaker animals are left behind. The male or female tiger then runs, jumps on a buffalo's back and bites it. After some time, the buffalo is in so much pain that it falls down. Once the animal falls down the whole family of tigers, including the cubs, comes to eat it, even though it's not yet dead. By now you could also have been like that.

Or by now you could have been one of those lobsters in a glass tank in a restaurant. You could have been there right now. Some businessman could come along and, pointing at you, say, "I want that one!" Somebody with gloves would then put you into boiling hot water. It would make you scream for a few seconds, then that would be it. So, by now you could also have been like that.

Besides being born as a being in the lower realms, even if you were born as a human, you could have been born as an ordinary human being. You would never have met Dharma; you wouldn't have a single understanding of Dharma. You would have had no opportunity to practice Dharma in your whole life, even if you lived for seventy or even a hundred years. If you had been born like that, even though you were a human being, you would have had no opportunity at all to learn Dharma, let alone practice it. You would have no opportunity to acquire Dharma wisdom. You couldn't bear that ordinary human being's life, even though it's a human life. You would totally misunderstand the cause of happiness and the cause of suffering. Even if you did some intellectual study, your knowledge of the causes of happiness and suffering would be totally wrong.

Even though you would be a human being, you couldn't bear that life even for one day. You couldn't stand even for one day to be a human being with no knowledge of Dharma and no opportunity to practice it.

It's very good to picture yourself in those situations and imagine how it would be, because it then makes you appreciate your present perfect human body. That you have met the Dharma and taken the opportunity to follow the teachings is like a dream. It's an incredibly joyful thing. But you also shouldn't waste it. Not practicing Dharma with this perfect human body for a minute, or even a second, is an incredible waste. It's a greater loss than losing zillions of dollars. Wasting this precious human body by not practicing Dharma for a minute, or even a second, is a greater loss than having lost billions of zillions of dollars or the whole sky filled with wish-granting jewels.

You might be doing Medicine Buddha meditation in your daily life or just to help Peter at this difficult time. It is a most critical time, with either the possibility to be born in the realm of a happy trans-migratory being or the incredible danger, because of all the past negative karmas, of being born in the lower realms.

When you yourself have died, with your breath stopped, you reach the intermediate state on your journey to the lower realms; the intermediate state of one of the lower realms appears. Even while you're in the intermediate state, there are terrifying karmic appear-ances of burning fires, winds like tornadoes, violent waves, moun-tains crushing you and so forth. These terrifying visions, even in the intermediate state, are the appearances of negative karma; they are the results of delusions, of the impure mind.

The times while you are dying and when you are recently dead are most critical. You need so much help at those times. If somebody from the human realm is praying for you, that is very kind. You have incredible need of that help. So there is no doubt about your need of prayers if you have already been born in the lower realms and are experiencing the most unbearable, unimaginable suffering. Use yourself as an example; think of your being in that situation. So, you must pray for Peter. Whenever you hear that a student in the FPMT organization has passed away, you must dedicate your merits to them or do your best prayers for them. This applies in general, not only to when an FPMT student has died. You should do this when you're watching the news on TV or reading the newspapers and you see that many people have died. Just one or two days ago, thirty thousand people died in an earthquake in Iran. A whole city, built in the traditional way with mud, was completely destroyed by the earthquake. Whenever you see something like that on TV, you should immediately pray, "Due to all the merits of the three times collected by me and by others, may all of these people who have died be born in a pure land of buddha where they can be enlightened or receive a perfect human body, meet a perfectly qualified Mahayana guru and Mahayana teachings and achieve enlightenment as quickly as possible." You must immediately pray in this way. Don't just think, "I'll pray for them later." Do it immediately. As soon as you hear someone has died, pray for them. This is our duty, our responsibility, our job.

It's also very good to immediately recite some OM MANI PADME HUM's or some other mantra for anyone who has died. Pray for them and then recite some mantras.

ABANDONING LAZINESS

In relation to abandoning laziness so that your life isn't spent being distracted by meaningless things, a text mentions:

> One who is craving small pleasure cannot achieve the great pleasure.

Anyone who clings to small pleasures won't achieve the great pleasure, which means the everlasting happiness of liberation from samsara. Craving samsaric pleasure, which doesn't last, itself becomes an obstacle to achieving the great pleasure of everlasting happiness, which never changes, never decreases. After you have removed even the seed of delusion, the imprint that gives rise to delusion, motivates karma and results in all the sufferings of samsara, there's then no cause to give rise to delusion, no cause for suffering. When that happens, since it's impossible for you to suffer again, you experience everlasting happiness, including the peerless happiness of full enlightenment, which is complete bliss.

By craving small happiness, small pleasure, you cannot achieve the great pleasure of liberation from samsara and full enlightenment. It becomes an obstacle to that. If you wish to achieve the everlasting happiness of liberation from samsara and full enlightenment, you have to let go of small pleasures. You can't have both, just as you can't sew with a two-pointed needle. If you put one leg on one road and the other on another road, you can't proceed. You can't go on two different paths at the same time. So, if your goal is to achieve liberation from samsara or full enlightenment, you have to let go of the desire clinging to small pleasures. In order to achieve this great pleasure, the everlasting happiness of total liberation from the whole ocean of samsaric suffering and its causes and especially to achieve the everlasting happiness of full enlightenment, you have to give up the small pleasures of this life. There is no doubt that you have to give up the comforts of this life, but you even have to give up all samsaric pleasures, which are transitory. Your mind has simply labeled "pleasure" on a suffering feeling, and that pleasure doesn't even last.

This quotation is also advice about not being lazy. When you crave small pleasures, you become lazy. You have to let go of those small pleasures because it means giving up the great pleasure of liberation from samsara and full enlightenment.

ABANDONING ATTACHMENT

I'd like to say a little more on what I talked about last night. As I mentioned last night, seeing a person, or their body, as an object of desire is a creation of your own mind. And so is seeing someone as an object of anger. If you understand how an object of desire is the creation of your mind, you will know that any object of anger also simply comes from your mind. It's a creation of your mind, a projection of your mind.

How you see someone, how you see someone's body, is the view of your mind. Their appearance came from your mind; it's a projection of your mind, of your present concept. The kind of concept you have at the moment you see that person's body creates that appearance. If your concept labels them "ugly," they then appear ugly to you. If you label them "beautiful," you then have an appearance of beauty after your mind has labeled, or interpreted, in that way. This is just your own view, the view of your present concept, your present way of thinking. When you realize this, you then know there's nothing from the side of the person or their body. Attachment arises through believing there's something coming from outside, from the side of the person or their body. On the basis of that belief, attachment arises.

When something appears ugly to you and anger arises or something appears beautiful and attachment arises, you should think, "This is my own view, my own projection. This appearance happened as a result of what my mind has labeled." When you think in this way, attachment then feels shy. There's no place for attachment; it disappears. You don't see any purpose in giving rise to attachment, in being attached to anything.

Last night I mentioned that there's also a long-term evolution of your view of a person or their body, which involves past karma. The past karmic imprint left on your mental continuum projects your view of the person. I gave the example of how even though many people may see someone's body as ugly, one person may see that person's body as beautiful. I also gave the example of how you may have been seeing someone's body for a long time but not seen them as beautiful; but then suddenly one day they appear to you to be beautiful. On that day your karmic imprint from the past manifests and projects, or creates, this view of that person as beautiful, and attachment then arises. It is like images on a film. When you put the film into a projector, those images are then projected onto a movie or TV screen. In a similar way, your past karmic imprint today projects this view of the person as beautiful and you see them as beautiful; attachment then arises and clings to that object.

Another example of how the object of anger, attachment or jealousy is the projection of your own mind is mentioned in the Madhyamaka teachings. This particular example is very useful in many places, including in guru devotion, when as a disciple you're trying to have the realization that the guru is a buddha. It is also useful in relation to respecting others. When I explain the example you will understand how it helps you to respect others. Throughout your whole life, the view that you have is that of your own mind. If your mind is pure, you have a pure view; if your mind is impure, the view that you have is impure. Here, again, we can use the example of projecting a film: whether violence or enjoyment is projected on the movie or TV screen depends on what is on the film.

The example is that there's one bowl of liquid. When pretas, who have no merit to see anything of better quality, see this bowl of liquid, the liquid appears to them as pus and blood. This is their view of the liquid, and it came from their mind. Pretas have no merit, no good karma, to see anything better than this. They see neither water, which is what we humans see, nor nectar, which is what the devas, the worldly gods, see. When we look at that same liquid, we see water and at the same time, when devas look at the liquid, they see nectar. Pretas don't have the merit to see either water or nectar. Because of their lack of merit and impure mind, they see only impure substances, pus and blood, when they look at that bowl of liquid. All three types of beings are the same in seeing a liquid, but this liquid appears to pretas as pus and blood, because of their lack of merit, their impure mind. The same liquid appears as water to us human beings. Since we have a little more merit, the liquid appears as water rather than pus and blood. When devas look at this same bowl of liquid, because they have more merit, it appears to them as nectar.

There is one object, one bowl of liquid, but it appears differently to the different beings in dependence upon how pure their mind is and how much merit they have. You can now see that how the object appears completely depends on the quality of the perceiver's mind, on how pure or impure it is.

This example is very helpful in guru devotion. There are four main reasons to prove that the guru is a buddha, the last of which is *nothing is definite in my view*. You can't use the fact that the guru appears to you to have faults as a reason to prove that in reality the guru has faults, because how an object appears to you is totally dependent on your, the perceiver's, mind.

There is also a story about a butcher who visited the Jokhang, the main temple in Lhasa, where there's the most precious statue of Shakyamuni Buddha, which was built during Buddha's time under Buddha's direction. An artist, who was a manifestation, made this statue for Buddha's mother, because she missed Buddha so much when he went to the Realm of the Thirty-three for *yar-ne*, the summer retreat. The statue was made on Buddha's instructions for his mother, so that she could look at the statue of Buddha during

Buddha's absences. Buddha predicted that this statue would be in India and benefit many sentient beings there for a certain number of years, then it would go to Mongolia and benefit many sentient beings there for a certain period. The statue would then go to China and benefit many sentient beings there for a certain number of years. It would then go to the Snow Land, Tibet, and benefit many sentient beings there for a certain period. And it would then go to the *naga* land, which, I think, means under the ocean.

When the butcher went to the Lhasa temple to see this statue of Buddha, he couldn't see the statue at all. He couldn't see even the butter lamps around the statue. It was totally dark. It wasn't because of his eyes. You might think that Tibetans don't know anything and that he must have had cataracts or something else wrong with his eyes, but it wasn't because of anything like that. He went to see a lama, who told him to do many hundreds of thousands of prostrations by reciting the Thirty-five Buddhas' names. After doing that, he still couldn't see the statue, but he could see the lights.

Another person went to receive teachings from a lama, who was giving an oral transmission of a text. The person, who must have had heavy negative karma, could not see the text. During all those hours of oral transmission, he saw only piles of meat and the lama eating that meat. That was all he saw. When the mind is obscured by heavy negative karma, you can't even see statues of Buddha or holy texts.

Now, here, the same liquid appeared differently, as pure or impure, to different beings, according to the quality of their mind. You can see that the appearance of pus and blood, water or nectar came from the perceiver's mind. You can understand very easily that their view came from their mind; it was a production of their mind. It depended on the amount of their merit and the purity of their mind.

Now it is the same in our daily life. In exactly the same way, our objects of anger and attachment come from our mind. We normally think that something comes from the object's side, that there's something real from its own side, which then causes anger or attachment to arise. That appearance and that belief are totally wrong. I already described this yesterday in relation to Lama Tsong-khapa quoting from the commentary to *Four Hundred Stanzas*, and I don't want to repeat it.

This analysis of our perception makes it even clearer that there is nothing from the object's side. That object of anger or attachment comes from the side of our mind; it is what our mind has projected. This is what we should remember, this is what we should meditate on. We should practice mindfulness of this when we see we're in danger of giving rise to attachment or anger in relation to objects. We should be aware of when we are in a situation where it is about to happen. As *Eight Verses of Thought Transformation* says:

> I will examine my own mental continuum in all actions, and the moment I realize a delusion is arising, endangering myself and others, I will diligently practice to avert it in the quickest, most powerful way.

Attachment endangers you and others, causing you to create negative karma, and you then cause others to engage in negative karma.

It is the same with anger and the other delusions. It makes you and others evil. How does it make you evil? By giving rise to the evil mind of delusion, you then engage in evil actions, which result only in suffering and are obstacles to achieving happiness for yourself and others, especially liberation and enlightenment.

The more you delay applying the meditation, the more you destroy your enlightenment, your liberation and all your happiness, not only of this life but of future lives. You destroy so many eons of merits. As *A Guide to the Bodhisattva's Way of Life* says:

> Giving rise to anger for one second destroys the merit collected by having made offerings to the buddhas, made charity and so forth for one thousand eons.[25]

The more you delay applying meditation, the greater destruction of your own happiness, of your own merit, there is.

You should immediately meditate in the following way. Think, "This is my view. This object that I'm attached to (or angry with) comes from my mind. This appearance has come through my mind labeling." The other point to consider is karma. Think, "There's nothing there from the side of the object—this is just the appearance of my karmic imprint. The object I'm attached to (or angry with) is an appearance created by my own mind, so it's totally childish to be attached to (or angry with) it. It's total nonsense." It's like a child who has built a sand castle; when somebody then destroys it the child gets so upset, screaming, "You destroyed my house!"

[25] Ch. 6, v. 1

Like this child who gets so angry and cries so much, you get angry with the appearance that your mind created. That appearance came about through your mind labeling it. Your past karmic imprint projected this view, then you got angry with or attached to it. Your thinking is totally opposite to the reality. You think that appearance is coming from outside, from the object's side, which is totally false. That's a hallucination.

A great Kagyü yogi, Gyalwa Götsangpa, said:

> Others' mistakes are your own mistakes. Therefore, visualize the appearance of mistakes as your *yidam*.

The advice here is to change the mistaken appearance you have into pure appearance, as in tantric practice. Gyalwa Götsangpa says that when we see others' mistakes, they're our mistakes. When somebody cheats you, lies to you, gets angry with you or abuses you, remember what Gyalwa Götsangpa says : *Others' mistakes are your own mistakes.*

The bodies of Mahayana arya beings—the exalted beings who have actualized the Mahayana path of seeing or path of meditation and have the wisdom directly perceiving emptiness—are not like our bodies. Since they have abandoned the sufferings of rebirth, old age, sickness and death, even if others try to harm them, there's no pain. Because of their level of purification, they don't experience pain in the way we do; through having actualized the path, they have ceased a certain level of obscurations, though not necessarily all of the obscurations. Since Mahayana arya beings don't experience pain, there is no doubt about buddhas, who have totally removed even the subtle negative imprints that project truly existent appearance. Even when millions of maras tried to attack Shakyamuni Buddha, all the weapons that they threw were transformed into flowers, so Buddha didn't receive any harm. Even before becoming a buddha, a bodhisattva who has attained the path of seeing or the path of meditation doesn't experience pain. That comes about through development of the mind, through having purified negative karma and defilements.

We receive harm and feel pain because we haven't purified our mind. Receiving harm and experiencing pain are totally dependent on whether we have or have not purified our mind. It's totally dependent on our mind. Somebody hurting us mentally by insulting us or hurting us physically by hitting us has to do with our mind. If we have purified our mind, if we have actualized those levels of the path, we cannot experience pain at all. This is especially so if we have reached the completion stage of the tantric path—the stages of clear light and illusory body. Once we reach those stages, we don't experience pain. Even if we fall down or somebody hits us with a stick, we don't feel pain; we feel only bliss. Kirti Tsenshab Rinpoche recently explained this when giving a commentary on the tantric grounds and paths.

Another proof comes from the great meditator, Gen Jampa Wangdu. Many of you have heard of Gen Jampa Wangdu, one of the old meditators from Dharamsala and Dalhousie from whom many of the older FPMT Sangha received the practice of *chu-len*, or taking the essence, the pill retreat. If you want to live in a remote, isolated place for many years to do retreat on calm abiding or meditate on the path, and you have to go very far to get food, with this practice you can just live on pills. Gen Jampa Wangdu himself lived on these pills and accomplished the practice.

One time we were receiving teachings from His Holiness the Dalai Lama, who was giving the teaching in the palace, not in the main temple. One morning there was a lot of rain, and the cement steps outside the palace had become very wet. During the break Gen Jampa Wangdu slipped and fell, hitting his head on the steps. After the teaching was finished, we both went back to Tushita Retreat Centre and talked a little together. He mentioned that he had slipped over and hit his head. He told me that when he hit his head on the steps he felt much bliss. He didn't experience any pain, just bliss. When he came inside there was a little blood on his head. I didn't see it happen, but His Holiness blew on Gen Jampa Wangdu's wound.

Gen Jampa Wangdu didn't become a traditional geshe, where you have to make big offerings. There are different levels of the geshe degree. Some monks are examined and answer questions, then get the degree. Those who are unable to give the answers can instead recite many pages of texts by heart. However, even though Gen Jampa Wangdu didn't do any of those examinations, he was a real geshe.

He actualized bodhicitta in Dharamsala many years ago. Sometimes in the evenings, after the teachings or at other times, he would come to see Lama Yeshe and me, and we would chat. Gen Jampa Wangdu would tell us stories. Some meditators would offer their realizations to His Holiness the Dalai Lama and others, whose root guru was His Holiness Trijang Rinpoche, would go to see Trijang

Rinpoche and explain what they had achieved. When Gen Jampa Wangdu went to see His Holiness, His Holiness would then tell him the news of the realizations achieved by the meditators, some of whom wrote to His Holiness from remote places. Gen Jampa Wangdu could go to see His Holiness without going through the Private Office for an appointment. The only time he went through the office was when I wanted to request His Holiness to give Gyalwa Gyatso initiation; he then went through the Tibetan secretary to make the request to His Holiness. He told me that this was the only time he went through the office.

Since Gen Jampa Wangdu had achieved calm abiding and also the Six Yogas of Naropa, he had clairvoyance. Because of this, I think he could see whether His Holiness had time to see him or not. Because he was clairvoyant, he could go straight to see His Holiness at any time. Maybe he sometimes had to wait a little while, but he never had to go through the office.

Also, at certain times when he was needed, Gen Jampa Wangdu would come to see us. When there was a need, he'd appear. He would go to see other people in a similar way—if somebody was dying with much suffering or difficulty, for example. Even though he would be in his cave, I think he was able to see what was happening. He would just go there to that dying person's house at the right time.

Anyway, Gen Jampa Wangdu told us, "For seven years I have never been in anybody's house for myself." It doesn't mean that he didn't go to other people's houses, but that he had generated bodhicitta seven years before. During that time, not only had he not gone to other people's houses for himself, but for seven years he hadn't done any activity for himself.

In Dharamsala Gen Jampa Wangdu lived for many years in a cave under a big rock, down below where His Holiness Ling Rinpoche lived on top of the hill. He realized emptiness there in that cave. He had already accomplished calm abiding in Dalhousie. After His Holiness sent Geshe Rabten to Dalhousie to inspire meditators to practice and achieve this realization, Gen Jampa Wangdu started to meditate on calm abiding and accomplished it. When he began the practice, he had a dream that he was riding a horse and that the horse fell down. He thought it was an inauspicious sign indicating that maybe he wouldn't achieve calm abiding; but I think it actually meant that he would be able to control the obstacles to single-pointed concentration, attachment-scattering thought and sinking thought.

Gen Jampa Wangdu used to stretch out his arms when he described the bliss that comes by achieving calm abiding. He used to say, "Until you achieve calm abiding, what you call meditation is not meditation." This is because we always have gross or subtle attachment-scattering thought or gross or subtle sinking thought. Gen Jampa Wangdu also had great success with the Six Yogas of Naropa. It was because he had reached those levels of the completion stage that though he fell heavily and knocked his head on the cement step, as Gen Jampa Wangdu explained, he experienced bliss instead of pain.

Let's put it this way: if you don't have negative karma, you don't experience pain.

Others' mistakes are your own mistakes. Therefore, visualize the appearance of mistakes as your yidam.

When somebody has abused you, insulted you, disrespected you,
cheated you, if you analyze the situation, you find that it is your
own mistake. Why? As great bodhisattva Shantideva mentions in
A Guide to the Bodhisattva's Way of Life, it is because your karma per-
suaded that person that you receive this harm.

> In the past, I gave similar harm to other sentient beings.
> Therefore, I deserve to receive this harm from other sentient
> beings.[26]

(I won't mention the other quotation that comes at the end of
the chapter and is about using how others treat you to develop
compassion.)[27]

Shantideva is saying that this person is treating you badly because
in the past you treated them in exactly the same way. Because you
harmed that person in that way in the past, you deserve to receive
harm from them at this time. *Deserve* means that you accept the situation rather than rejecting it by saying, "It's okay that I harmed
others in this way, but I can't receive the same harm from them."
It is unreasonable to reject it when others harm you but think it is

---

[26] Ch. 6, v. 42
[27] Therefore, just like treasure appearing in my house
Without any effort on my behalf to obtain it,
I should be happy to have an enemy
For he assists me in my conduct of awakening. Ch. 6, v. 107

fine for you to harm others. Saying *I deserve to receive this harm* means you are accepting your own mistake. The way that others harm you in this life is the result of how you treated them in the past, whether in past lives or earlier in this life. You can now see that when others treat you badly in this life, it is your own fault. As Gyalwa Göt-sangpa says, *Others' mistakes are your own mistakes.* When you relate this to karma, it's very clear.

Therefore, visualize the appearance of mistakes as your yidam means that you visualize the person who is harming you as a deity. With this meditation technique, anger and the other delusions do not arise.

I thought to bring up this issue of what Gyalwa Götsangpa said because even though we (and I include myself here) normally talk so much about karma, in our daily lives when we actually experience karma—when somebody treats us badly, insults, disrespects, abuses or cheats us—at that time we never think of karma. We think it's totally the fault of the other person, not our fault; we have never made any mistakes. We totally blame the other person.

This way of meditating, or analyzing, in which you make the discovery that it's your own mistake when others create negative karma in relation to you, becomes the practice of patience. Understanding this leads to the practice of patience because it's then impossible for you to give rise to anger.

The other point is that it inspires you to generate compassion. What is happening is not the other person's fault but your fault. Because you acted in this way toward others in the past, you obliged this person or these people to create negative karma by harming you in this way, which then causes them to be reborn in the lower realms. Who is throwing them into the lower realms? You. You're the one who causes them to fall from the human realm down into the lower realms. Therefore, these people who abuse you or harm you in other ways are purely objects of compassion. So, this verse helps you in two ways: it helps you to develop patience and is a powerful way to generate compassion.

I meant to finish *The Bodhisattva's Jewel Garland* this evening, but I got stuck at the beginning. I think we'll stop here. We're going to do the Gyalwa Gyatso initiation half in a dream or half alive....

> Due to all the past, present and future merits collected by me and the merits of the three times collected by others, which are empty from their own side, may the I, who is empty from its own side, achieve Compassion Buddha's enlightenment, which is empty from its own side, and lead all sentient beings, who are empty from their own side, to that enlightenment, which is empty from its own side, by myself alone, who is also empty from its own side.

Please also dedicate the merits in the following way.

> May the general teaching of Buddha and in particular the stainless teaching of Lama Tsongkhapa, which uni-fies sutra and tantra, be actualized in my own heart, in the hearts of the members of my family, of all of us here, of all the students and benefactors of the FPMT organization, especially those who give their lives to the organization,

offering service to sentient beings and the teaching of Buddha. In that way, may these teachings spread in all directions and flourish forever in this world.

January 1
PROTECTING YOURSELF

I just want to mention a few points in relation to the verse from *The Bodhisattva's Jewel Garland* where Lama Atisha is saying:

> With remembrance, awareness and conscientiousness,
> Always protect the door of your senses.
> Three times day and night, again and again,
> Examine your mental continuum.

Protecting yourself means protecting your own mind so that you don't engage in negative karmas of body, speech and mind. By allowing delusions to arise, you endanger yourself by creating negative karmas with your body, speech and mind, and you also endanger others. You harm others and you harm yourself, destroying your own happiness. You destroy not only today's or this moment's peace and happiness, but all the happiness of your future lives, including your own ultimate happiness of liberation from samsara and full enlightenment. It also becomes an obstacle to your actualizing the path and offering deep and extensive benefit to other sentient beings.

The other way to protect yourself is by not allowing yourself to be abused by your delusions, by your own ignorance, anger and attachment. You don't allow yourself to be harmed or destroyed by your enemy, delusions. If you follow your delusions, if you allow yourself to be controlled by your delusions, you then create negative karma, which means you throw yourself into the lower realms.

You may get upset when you suddenly remember that in your childhood you were abused by your father, your mother or somebody else, but at the moment you are being abused twenty-four hours a day by self-cherishing thought, ignorance, anger and attachment. You are being abused by these delusions all the time. This has been happening not only today but twenty-four hours a day since your birth and during beginningless rebirths. So, what are you going to do about it?

When you have abused somebody in the past and the result of that karma ripens so that you are now abused by that person, it makes you think you are the worst person in the world. You show an unbelievably sad face and say, "I'm hopeless." You may think you're worse than even an animal—worse than a mosquito, a flea or an ant. That comes from not having thought about and understood karma. It comes from not having reflected on Dharma and understood Dharma.

We're being abused all the time by self-cherishing thought, ignorance, anger, attachment and other delusions. There's no break from being abused by them. We need to recognize this and separate ourselves from delusions, rather than always being friends with them. Rather than being inseparable from our enemy, the delusions, we have to recognize how our delusions have been abusing us not only today but all the time from our birth and throughout beginningless rebirths. If we can generate the same feelings toward the delusions that we have toward a person who has abused us, it will inspire us and give us the courage not to follow our delusions but to defeat them. Instead of letting our delusions control us, we will control them. We will defeat our delusions, rather than letting them defeat us.

We aren't upset in the slightest about our real enemy, our delusions. We don't like anybody to dictate to us, but we're always being dictated to by our self-cherishing thought, by our ignorance, by our anger, by our attachment. They are the real dictators, always controlling us and never giving us any freedom.

This is another way of protecting yourself. Through this practice, you are freeing yourself from your enemy, delusions. You are giving freedom to yourself; you are giving peace to yourself away from the disturbance of the delusions. There are many different ways you can do this practice of controlling the delusions, and you are then giving liberation to yourself. In this way, because you don't create negative karma by giving rise to delusion, you are liberating yourself from the lower realms. This is the immediate danger. Death can happen at any time, and the immediate thing after that is the lower realms. Being free from that danger means that you have the opportunity to practice Dharma and gradually free yourself from samsara by actualizing the path.

NOTHING TO TRUST IN APPEARANCES

Yesterday I used the example of different beings seeing liquid in a container to explain the views of attachment and anger on seeing an object, such as someone's body. When you get attached to or angry with somebody, it doesn't come from the side of the object. You get attached to or angry with something that came only from your mind, to an appearance that is projected by your mind.

Yesterday, to clarify this, I used the example of how the same liquid in the same container appears differently to different beings in accord with the quality of the perceiver's mind. To those with an impure mind, to those without any merit, it appears impure, as pus, blood and other unpleasant things. To those with a pure mind it appears pure, as nectar. To the pretas, who don't have merit, it appears as only pus and blood. But when a human being looks at the same liquid at the same time it appears to them as water. When a worldly deva, who has more merit, looks at that same liquid in the same container, it appears as nectar. And, of course, for yogis and others who have pure appearance, and especially for buddhas, who have totally purified their holy minds, it appears as blissful, uncontaminated nectar.

Therefore, you can see that your view is a production of your own mind, just as these different beings see different things according to the different qualities of their minds. There's no such thing coming from the side of the object; there's no such thing existing from the side of the object without depending on the mind. To put it in the shortest way: there's no such thing from its own side. It's all appearance. All the objects that you see also come from your mind; they are the result of the quality of your mind.

This example is also very good to use in guru devotion and in respecting sentient beings. For example, even when you see a dog, the question is, "Is it a real dog or not?" Your seeing a dog doesn't always mean that it is a dog. Take Asanga, for example. Before Asanga had purified his mind, he saw Maitreya Buddha as a dog. But after he had purified his negative karma by generating incredible compassion and sacrificing himself for that one living being, the ordinary, impure appearance of Maitreya Buddha as a dog disappeared. The same being that had appeared before as a dog now appeared as a buddha.

You can't really say who is a buddha and who is not a buddha. When you see a beggar or an animal, you can't judge what they are from what appears to you. Saying "I see a dog" or "I see an ordinary being" doesn't logically prove that it is a dog or an ordinary being.

It also helps to remember what is mentioned in *The Essence of Nectar*:

> Until I am free from my evil karmic obscurations, even if all the buddhas descended in front of me, I have no fortune to see the holy body adorned with the holy signs and exemplifications—only this present appearance.[28]

We have no fortune to see buddhas in the aspect of buddha. We see only ordinary beings. The meaning of *ordinary* is having faults,

[28] See *Essential Nectar*, p. 193, v. 121.

delusions and suffering and making mistakes in actions. That's the definition of *ordinary*, as His Holiness the Dalai Lama explained during the *Guru Puja* commentary[29] that the FPMT requested as part of the Second Enlightened Experience Celebration in Dharamsala. Later, when I went for an interview, I mentioned to His Holiness that these words had benefited me very much.

Until our mind is separated from karmic obscurations, even if all the buddhas came in front of us, it doesn't mean that we would be able to see them as buddhas. We would see only ordinary beings with faults, or even animals.

If you're not sure whether a person or an animal is a buddha or a bodhisattva, your seeing them as an ordinary being with faults doesn't prove that they're an ordinary being. We definitely see buddhas, bodhisattvas and dakinis in our daily life in different places, especially in holy places. When we go to holy places such as the twenty-four holy places, there are numberless *dakas* and *dakinis* there, but it doesn't mean that we recognize them. When we are in cities or on pilgrimage, we do meet holy beings, but it doesn't mean that we recognize them. We cling strongly to our ordinary view, totally believing in it. Since we are habituated to our ordinary view, it blocks our seeing holy beings. Even if we see some special signs, it's still difficult for us to believe that it's a buddha and to really respect that being and behave toward them as it explains in the teachings. We don't follow them or make requests to them.

We certainly do meet buddhas, bodhisattvas, dakas and dakinis.

[29] Published as *The Union of Bliss and Emptiness*.

It's just that our heavy ordinary appearance and strong belief in our own view block our seeing that they are buddhas, bodhisattvas, dakas or dakinis. Because our mind is impure, our view of someone as ordinary doesn't prove that in reality they are like that.

Therefore, since anyone we meet could be a buddha, a bodhi-sattva, a daka or a dakini, we should respect everyone we meet. We should be careful not to get angry with or disrespect them, which creates heavy negative karma. By thinking that they might be a holy being, we should respect them and serve them, which creates so much merit. By thinking like this in our daily life, we gain a lot of advantages; we make a lot of profit, a lot of merit. The first thing is not to create negative karma, which is the obstacle for realizations and the cause of samsara, especially of the lower realms.

When the mind is not purified, it sees beings as ordinary. The stories of Asanga and the novice monk Kusali[30] are inspiring stories that show the benefit of generating great compassion and sac-rificing yourself for even one sentient being. It brings the quickest, most powerful purification and collection of merit and enables you to quickly achieve enlightenment. Although these stories also illus-trate the benefits of generating great compassion for even one sen-tient being, I'm using them here to show that our view of someone as pure or impure has totally to do with our own mind. It's a pro-duction of our own mind, depending on whether the mind itself is pure or impure.

The following story of Asanga is also helpful in relation to

[30] Getsul Tsembulwa, in Tibetan.

respecting sentient beings. After Asanga had spent twelve years in retreat on Maitreya Buddha, nothing had happened. It was only after he generated unbearable compassion and sacrificed himself to take care of a wounded dog that he was able to see Maitreya. The lower part of the dog's body was an open wound filled with maggots, and Asanga cut flesh from his own thigh and stretched it out on the ground as somewhere for the maggots to live. Because collecting the maggots with his fingers might have crushed them, Asanga then closed his eyes and went to pick up the maggots with the tip of his tongue. But he found that he couldn't reach them. When he then opened his eyes, he saw Maitreya Buddha.

Asanga saw Maitreya Buddha not only as a dog, but as a wounded one filled with maggots. He saw something very awful. It is similar with us in our daily life. We can never tell whether in reality someone's a sentient being just because we see them as a sentient being; they could also be a buddha. Even someone very ugly, awful or terrifying could be a buddha. Asanga didn't see even an ordinary human being but a dog, and even that, a dog with great suffering.

The other story is about Kusali, the Vajrayogini practitioner who went to the Vajrayogini pure land. Kusali's guru, Krishnacharya,[31] was going to the holy place called Oddiyana to engage in tantric conduct, the final part of tantric practice. It seems there are all different kinds of tantric conduct, in accordance with the individual person; there's not one particular fixed conduct. Chöden Rinpoche said that one monk in Ganden Monastery who was about to achieve

---

[31] Nagpo Chöpa, in Tibetan.

enlightenment and was engaged in tantric conduct built a huge house. There was no particular use for the house; he just built it.

On the road to Oddiyana Krishnacharya met an extremely ugly woman riddled with leprosy and oozing pus and blood. No one would dare to touch her. She asked Krishnacharya to pick her up and take her to the other side of the river, but he didn't pay any attention to her and went straight across the river.

After some time, his disciple, Kusali, a monk living in thirty-six vows, came by and saw this leper. The woman asked him, "Please carry me to the other side of the river. Please take me there." When Kusali saw the woman, he generated unbelievable compassion for her. Even though he was a monk and even though she was a leper oozing pus and blood, without any hesitation and with incredible compassion he lifted the woman onto his back. When he reached the middle of the river, she then appeared to him as Vajravarahi, not as an ordinary woman any more. She then took Kusali, in that same body, to Dakpa Khachö, the pure land of Vajrayogini, where he became enlightened.

Here, because of the unbearable compassion he generated for just one living being, Kusali completely sacrificed himself to take care of that being. This brought such powerful purification of his impure karma and defilements that, without crossing the whole river, when he reached the middle of the river, his view of that woman was only of a deity, Vajravarahi. She then took him straight to the pure land without his needing to die or go to the intermediate state or a next life. In that life, in that same body, he was able to go to the pure land of Vajrayogini.

Here, Kusali seeing an ordinary leper was the view of his impure mind. By purifying the impurities of his mind, he then had the pure view of her as a deity.

Another angle of this story is the importance of generating compassion as strongly as possible. The stronger you generate compassion, for even one living being, the quicker you are able to achieve enlightenment.

I'm using these stories to help you to understand that all the objects that you are attached to or get angry with in your daily life are your karmic view; they all come from your own karma. They're creations, productions, of your own karma. The view of things as ugly or undesirable manifests from your own karmic imprints, as does the view of any object of attachment. The view of something as desirable is also a creation of your own karmic imprint. It means that there's nothing there from the side of the object, from outside. What we normally believe is totally wrong. When attachment, anger or any other delusion arises, we normally believe that it doesn't come from our mind but from its own side. We think that the appearance of an object of attachment or anger exists from its own side or comes from outside, instead of thinking that it comes from our mind, that it is the view of our karmic imprint.

In conclusion, there are three points to consider. The first is that this moment's appearance of a friend, enemy or object of attachment comes from this moment's concept. Your mind merely imputes, or makes up, that label and believes in it, and it then appears to you. After you label it, it appears to you in that way; you see it in that way. So, this moment's appearance of things has to do with this moment's concept; it's a creation of this moment's way of thinking.

The second point is that the appearance of this friend, enemy or object of attachment is the production of karma. It came from the karmic imprint, which means it came from your own mind. Again, there's nothing from the side of the object.

Now I want to tell you about the third point. The truly existent friend, the truly existent enemy, the truly existent object of desire, the truly existent harm, the truly existent help and so forth don't come from their own side; they are projections of the negative imprints left on your mental continuum by past ignorance. This is the third point. There's nothing coming from the side of the object, as we normally believe in our daily lives. It's the total opposite.

These three points give you an idea of how your view of an object comes from your own mind. It's very important to do this meditation, this analysis, and use it in your daily life when you're in danger of giving rise to delusions. It proves how delusion is a wrong concept because there's no such object as it apprehends. In the case of ignorance, there's no phenomenon that exists from its own side. Every phenomenon exists by being merely imputed by the mind in relation to a valid base. Because a valid base exists, that phenomenon is merely imputed by the mind. Therefore, nothing exists from its own side. No phenomenon exists from its own side; all phenomena are totally empty. That's the reality. All these things appearing to us one after another as not merely labeled by the mind, as existing from their own side, are total hallucinations. They are totally false—not even an atom of them exists.

This analysis proves that this ignorance that apprehends things as existing from their own side is totally wrong. It proves that ignorance is a false mind. And it is the same with anger, attachment and any other delusion: they are all wrong concepts. A superstition is something that you believe when in reality no such thing exists. So, all delusions are superstitions.

CONTROLLING DELUSIONS

Remembering the deity

Yesterday I mentioned a quotation from the great Kagyü yogi, Gyalwa Götsangpa:

> Others' mistakes are your own mistakes. Therefore, visualize the appearance of mistakes as your yidam.

I want to clarify the second part, where he says that you visualize the appearance of mistakes as your yidam, your deity.

When somebody harms, cheats, abuses or provokes you, there are many thought-transformation methods you could use, but Gyalwa Götsangpa mentions visualizing the person as your yidam, your mind-sealed deity. When you visualize them as the deity, there's suddenly no way you can be angry. Your anger immediately disappears. It also stops your creating negative karma by harming them in return. It stops your insulting or beating them or doing other negative actions out of anger. Because there is no way you can give rise to anger, the negative actions that follow anger don't happen. When you think of the person as the deity, you also give rise to respect. There are many benefits in visualizing the person as your deity.

In a similar way, you can also look at that person as your guru and think that you are receiving the blessing of the guru or the deity. There is a thought-transformation practice where you look at sentient beings as your own guru. Anger and other negative thoughts do not then arise and instead respect arises. That might be the reason that in thought transformation you practice looking at sentient beings as your guru.

When someone is possessed by spirits and there's also a danger they will harm others, if you visualize that person as a deity, they calm down or are unable to harm anyone.

Remembering that the buddhas are always watching

There are other methods to control your mind when you're in danger of giving rise to delusions and of engaging in negative karma. Kadampa Geshe Kharak Gomchung gave the following advice:

> Whatever thoughts arise in your mind, the buddhas' holy mind can always see them. Since the buddhas' holy mind is clear, without obscuration, it can see what you are thinking. There are numberless buddhas, and all the time they can clearly see what you are thinking. When you give rise to attachment, anger and other negative thoughts, the buddhas see what is going on in your mind.

Because numberless buddhas see what you're thinking, when attachment and other negative thoughts arise, you should remember,

"All the buddhas are watching me. They can see my mind; they can see that I'm generating negative thoughts." You will then suddenly feel embarrassed and want to stop thinking of that object of delusion and following that delusion. This is what happens when you remember that since the holy mind of all the buddhas is clear, without obscuration, they see everything that's going on, including when you're generating delusions. You will then feel embarrassed that you are doing something wrong, and that will help you to control the delusion or at least to control your responses.

Kharak Gomchung then says:

> Don't let bad thoughts run in your mind, because it upsets your yidam.

For example, if you display bad manners in front of respected people, they will think you are disrespectful or stupid. Or if somebody who has become your friend finds out that you are selfish and have other bad traits, they will think badly of you. First they respect and like you, then later, when they find out about all your faults and all the bad things you have done, they get upset and see you as bad.

Kharak Gomchung then explains that, like someone with sight watching a blind person, the buddhas are always looking at what you're thinking and how you're behaving. The blind person doesn't realize that people with sight can see all the mistakes they are making, such as going where there's no road or where there's danger. In a similar way, without obscuration, the buddhas and bodhisattvas are always watching you and seeing your mistakes.

Kharak Gomchung then continues:

Therefore, don't get excited about engaging in bad behavior.

Kharak Gomchung is giving us a technique to help us control our mind. When we suddenly remember that all the buddhas are watching us, that they know about our mind and our bad behavior, we don't dare to continue. We have to stop. Being aware of the buddhas watching is one technique to control the mind.

Remembering the negative imprints

Another technique is to think of the negative imprints. Whenever attachment, anger, heresy or any other delusion arises, it's not simply arising but leaving a negative imprint on your mental continuum, like planting a seed in a field. As you have more and more negative thoughts and perform more and more negative actions, more and more negative imprints are left on your mental continuum, which make your coming future lives more and more difficult. In your future lives, because those negative thoughts and actions left negative imprints on your mental continuum, because of this past habituation, it then becomes very difficult for you to stop negative behavior. For example, if you are habituated to stealing, as more negative imprints are left by those thoughts and actions of stealing, it becomes more difficult for you to stop stealing in your future lives. Stealing happens uncontrollably. It is the same with sexual misconduct and all other negative actions. Because of the negative imprints left in this life, it becomes difficult for you to stop negative actions, making your future lives very difficult. Also, because you have already left so many negative imprints in your past lives, delusions arise and make you do negative actions, which then leave more negative imprints, which then make it very difficult in future lives for you to control your mind and to stop these bad behaviors. Again you leave negative imprints on your mind. This happens continuously, creating obstacles and obscuring your mind, making your life very difficult. The negative imprints left on your mind by attachment and other negative thoughts and by negative actions harm you in many, many lifetimes. It goes on and on in that way. With hell, you experience it for a certain length of time, then exhaust the karma to be in hell; but with a negative imprint left on the mind, you experience it again and again, until it is purified. Experiencing it again and again means you experience a difficult life and engage in those negative actions again and again.

Gungtang Rinpoche, a great Amdo lama, said:

> The evil friend, the friend of negative karma, isn't somebody who has horns growing on his head or who says, "I'm the friend of negative karma." He smiles at you in an affectionate, caring manner.

The friend of negative karma is the person who helps you to engage in careless activities, who helps you to play, laugh and be distracted.

> Abandon that friend of negative karma like a contagious disease. Abandon the nonvirtuous friend, who is like a smiling cannibal or the *hala* plant.

At the beginning, when you first meet a cannibal, he smiles, says, "I love you," "I care for you" and many other nice things and shows you a lot of affection, but later, when you have come believe in what he says, he eats you—by believing in the cannibal, you are cheated: afterwards, he eats you.

Similarly, the *hala* plant has a beautiful flower but it's poisonous when you smell or eat it. Again, it cheats and harms you.

Another piece of advice from Kharak Gomchung, which is related to a verse from Lama Atisha's teaching, is:

> If the desire arises to engage in an unrighteous action, restrain your body and speech from engaging in it, from moving toward it. The advantage of doing that is that you eliminate obstacles for yourself and for others.

It eliminates obstacles for both self and others when you stop engaging in negative karma. When you don't stop engaging in negative karma, that itself is creating obstacles in your life. It creates obstacles to your Dharma practice, as well as to your health, so that you experience sicknesses. It creates obstacles to many things. It causes obstacles to you and to other people; there are problems in your life and in the lives of others. However, abstaining from engaging in unrighteous actions with your body and speech eliminates obstacles to self and to others. That itself becomes a puja—the best puja. In our daily life, whenever there's a danger of our engaging in unrighteous actions, such as when desire arises, we have to stop our body and speech from engaging in them. When we stop that, the puja is already done. Without needing to ask other people to do a puja for us, we ourselves have done the puja, because we stopped creating negative karma.

Kharak Gomchung then concludes:

> You will then receive the common *siddhis* and sublime realization.

One point is to remember to generate fear of negative imprints. Allowing delusions to arise and engaging in negative actions leave negative imprints. Remember how these imprints will also continuously harm you in your coming future lives. It is very important to be cautious of this. These pieces of advice from Kharak Gomchung are very powerful.

There are two main methods to control the mind. One, for us beginners, is to separate ourselves from the object of desire. Since we don't have realizations or a stable mind, being close to an object of desire is very dangerous for us. But even if we are physically separate from the object, if we don't meditate, it becomes very difficult because the desire is still there, clinging to the object. Even though physically we're far from the object, since mentally we didn't let go of the object, the suffering becomes unbearable. Therefore, not only do we need to be distant from the object, but at the same time we need to practice meditation. If the problem is anger, we need to meditate on the shortcomings of anger. We have to remember again and again all the suffering that results from anger. We need to meditate on the shortcomings as extensively as possible: anger results in the sufferings of the lower realms; and even when we are next born as a human being, we will have an ugly body and many other problems. If the problem is desire, meditate on the shortcomings of desire. It's not enough just to be physically distant from the object of desire. We need medicine for our mind. Desire is a sickness of the mind, and we need to take the medicine of meditation for it.

Yesterday and the other day I mentioned various other techniques for controlling the mind. One is to remember that death can happen at any time and relate that to negative karma and the sufferings of the lower realms. Relate in particular to the shortcomings of desire and of the negative actions done out of desire, which become nonvirtues. This is powerful and most effective. You need to reflect on those parts of the meditation, and on how samsara is suffering in nature.

There is a story of a person who was born without a right arm for five hundred lifetimes. After five hundred lifetimes, he was then born with a right arm. The karmic story is that in a past life the person was a monk who touched a woman's body with attachment then broke his vows. Because of that, he was born for five hundred lifetimes without a right arm. After five hundred lifetimes, because the karma had been exhausted, he was then born with a right arm. When he got the arm, he must have felt that it was very precious.

There are also many children born in different parts of the world as Siamese twins, with their bodies joined at the head, stomach or back. I think that many of those births are the result of strong desire. It could be that they took ordination in the past and broke their vows because of desire. These people could have been born like this because of very strong desire, not being able to let go of the object of desire. After that lifetime, they are then born with their stomachs, backs, lower bodies or heads joined. Recently in the news there was the story of a successful operation in America to separate two children. There was also a recent operation done in Singapore to separate twins joined at the head, but both of them died. They weren't small children, but quite grown up. I don't know how they were able to live like that for so many years. They decided to have the operation but neither of them survived.

In this text there are quotations from the sutras and many other karmic stories. Kachen Yeshe Gyaltsen, the great pandit, also has many karmic stories in his *Great Thought Transformation* text.

An ordinary being, who doesn't have realizations or a stable mind, needs to do strong meditation because their mind is very weak. They need to be far away from the object of desire, the object of delusion, and at the same time do strong meditation. Their mind then won't suffer as much, and they will be able to continue their practice; they will also be able to continue to live in their precepts or ordination.

Lama Zopa Rinpoche at Root Institute

Todd Moore

Kadampa Teachings 3

BODHGAYA, DECEMBER 2006

Geshe Langri Thangpa (1054–1123)

Jerry Powers

···Kadampa Teachings 3···

December 30

I'LL JUST READ THROUGH this teaching from Lama Atisha, *The Bodhisattva's Jewel Garland*. After the title, *The Bodhisattva's Jewel Garland*, it mentions how Lama Atisha is from India. It then says:

> I prostrate to great compassion.
> I prostrate to the gurus.

I prostrate to the gurus is *lama nam la chhag tshäl lo* in Tibetan. *Lama* is not used here in the way it's used in India, where all Tibetan men are called "lama," even the Tibetan police. I've never heard Indians call a Tibetan woman "lama," but any Tibetan man is called "lama." I think it might also be the same in Nepal.

Here *lama* refers to the guru and means very heavy with qualities. The ultimate meaning of *very heavy with qualities* is the dharmakaya, as I mentioned yesterday when I was talking about what the guru is and how you should think when you see or think about the guru or say the word "guru." (See appendix 3.) The dharmakaya, the wisdom of the fully enlightened mind, is free from all the disturbing-thought obscurations and subtle obscurations; not even the slightest trace of a fault is left on the mind. The dharmakaya is the one that manifests everything; it is where all the buddhas, all the Dharma and all the Sangha come from. The dharmakaya guides you through the conventional guru, by manifesting through the conventional guru. You can now understand that here *very heavy with qualities* means the dharmakaya, the ultimate perfection of wisdom. This is what manifests to guide you. So, you prostrate to the lamas, or gurus.

I prostrate to the devotional deity.

I'm not completely sure but this might mean your own personal deity, the one that you practice being one with in your daily life.

ABANDONING DOUBT

Abandon all doubts;
Definitely cherish the practice.

In one way it's good to have doubts, especially at the beginning, because your doubts can make you clarify and discover what's right. However, when you're traveling, if you have doubts about whether a road will lead you to where you want to go, you'll be unhappy about using it. Your doubts will stop you from taking that road. If it's the wrong road, it's okay; but if it's the correct one that leads to the place you want to go, your doubts will stop you from taking that road.

Here, having doubts about Buddha, Dharma and Sangha or about the path stops you from entering the path to liberation and enlightenment. Therefore, to engage in the path to liberation and enlightenment, you have to abandon doubts, because they're obstacles. So, you *abandon all doubts* and *definitely cherish the practice.*

ABANDONING SLEEP, DROWSINESS AND LAZINESS

Thoroughly abandon sleep, drowsiness and laziness.

Drowsiness means your mind becoming dark, like a dark house, when you meditate. Your mind is not clear, but dark. The Tibetan expression *rab pang* means to thoroughly abandon. Why do you have to thoroughly abandon sleep, drowsiness and laziness? Because they waste your life. They waste this most precious human life, with which you can achieve the three great meanings. If you have achieved a perfect human rebirth, which has eighteen qualities, with that you can then achieve the three great meanings. You can achieve any temporary happiness you wish, and at the time of death you can go to a pure land of buddha, from where you don't have to be reborn in the lower realms at all and you can achieve enlightenment. That means that in a future life you can achieve a perfect human rebirth and a human rebirth that has the eight ripening qualities highly admired by Lama Tsongkhapa.[32] You need to achieve a human body with the eight ripening aspects so that you

[32] The eight ripening qualities are 1) long life, 2) an attractive body, 3) high caste, 4) wealth, 5) trustworthy speech, 6) power and fame, 7) a male body and 8) a strong body and mind.

can make quick progress in attaining the realizations of the path to enlightenment. There's also the human rebirth with seven qualities: high caste, a beautiful body, long life, good health, wealth, power and wisdom. In countries with castes, if you are from a high caste, since everybody respects you, you can then benefit others. There is also the human rebirth with the four Mahayana Dharma wheels: you are born in the right family or right environment, which means there is no obstacle to your accepting the Dharma; the place where you practice is healthy and not harmful; you actualize the prayers you made in the past; and you are able to collect merit.

The other two great meanings are the ultimate happiness of liberation and of enlightenment.

By practicing Dharma, even within each second you can achieve any of these three great meanings that you wish to achieve; but you don't achieve these things if you don't abandon sleep, drowsiness and laziness.

It says here to abandon sleep, and there are some meditators who don't sleep at all. However, the lam-rim teachings usually say that the first part of the night is not for sleeping but for practice; the later part of the night is when you get up to practice; and the middle part of the night is the only time for sleeping. So, you have to look for the middle part of the night. Since I don't practice that, I don't really know how to find the middle part. My sleeping happens at totally the wrong time.

Abandoning sleep, drowsiness and laziness is very important. You have an unbelievable opportunity to achieve incredible things for yourself and for other sentient beings. You can bring happiness—the happiness of all their future lives, liberation from samsara and enlightenment—to so many sentient beings, numberless sentient beings, through your Dharma practice. If sleep, drowsiness and laziness become obstacles, you then lose all these things, including the perfect human rebirth with which you can achieve all of them.

We have this perfect human rebirth almost only this one time; it doesn't last long; and it can be stopped at any time. Therefore, if we spend the little time that we have in sleep, drowsiness and laziness, just attached to the pleasures of this life, we can't achieve realization. We can't achieve enlightenment, nor liberation from samsara, nor even the happiness of future lives.

HAVING PERSEVERANCE

Next Lama Atisha says:

Always attempt to have perseverance.

Before, it says that we should thoroughly abandon sleep, drowsiness and laziness. We should then always attempt to have perseverance. The nature of the mental factor of perseverance is a mind that is happy to perform virtue. Perseverance in harming your enemies, perseverance in anger, attachment or ignorance, perseverance in meaningless activities of this life or perseverance in nonvirtuous actions is not the real perseverance; that's wrong perseverance. The mind that is happy to create negative karma is wrong perseverance.

Here, *Always attempt to have perseverance* means having perseverance in virtue, in Dharma, in attaining the path. Understanding buddha-nature can help encourage you to have perseverance. Also, knowing how this perfect human body is so precious and that with it you can achieve all these great meaning helps you to have perseverance in practicing Dharma, in achieving the three great meanings.

Also, every day you should remember that negative karmas such as the ten nonvirtues result in the sufferings of the hell beings, hungry ghosts and animals. As Nagarjuna advises, to keep our mind always in virtue we should remember every day the sufferings of heat and cold of the hell realms. To keep a horse on the right path you hit it with a whip. If the horse goes off to the right or left, you hit it with the whip to keep it on the correct path. To always keep your mind in virtue, remember the unbelievable sufferings of the lower realms. That then gives you the courage and perseverance to bear hardships to practice Dharma, to attain the path to liberation and to enlightenment. Remembering those sufferings persuades you to take the lay vows—the five lay vows or the eight vows, such as the Eight Mahayana Precepts—and to bear hardships to purify negative karma and to collect merit and thus achieve liberation and enlightenment. It persuades you to do the various practices of purification to purify all your negative karmas, which cause you to be born in the lower realms, and also persuades you to attain the path, to engage in the practice of Dharma to have a good rebirth in future lives, so that you can again meet and practice the Dharma, and then complete the path to liberation and enlightenment. In that way you get inspired, and you have courage and perseverance. You should also remember how samsara and samsaric perfections are suffering in nature.

Another point is compassion. You feel it is unbearable that

sentient beings are suffering so much only if you have strong compassion for others. If you have that kind of mind, you also want to help others; you want to free others from their suffering and its causes and bring them to enlightenment. Feeling that others' sufferings are unbearable also gives you courage and perseverance to practice Dharma.

HAVING REMEMBRANCE, AWARENESS AND CONSCIENTIOUSNESS

Lama Atisha then says:

> With remembrance, awareness and conscientiousness,
> Always protect the doors of your senses.
> Three times day and night, again and again,
> Examine your mental continuum.

In *A Guide to the Bodhisattva's Way of Life*, Shantideva gives the following example. You have to walk while carrying a container filled with some precious drink. There's a person next to you holding a sword, and if you spill the drink, that person will strike you with the sword. So, while you're walking you watch the road but you also watch the container, so that you don't spill the drink. If you don't do that, you could be in danger.[33]

One simple example of this is always keeping your mind in lam-rim, in virtue, in daily life. If you don't keep your mind in virtue

[33] Chapter 7, v. 71

with remembrance, awareness and conscientiousness, there's a danger you will engage in negative karma. Negative thoughts will arise, and you will then create negative karma. You will then fall down into the lower realms for many eons of suffering. Even later, when you're again born as a human being due to another good karma, you will also experience much suffering in the human realm. You will reincarnate again and again in samsara, experiencing all the sufferings of samsara. Conscientiousness makes you pay attention, like the person being threatened by someone holding a sword.

You can have conscientiousness if you have remembrance and awareness. Remembrance means keeping your mind in virtue; keeping your mind in guru devotion, renunciation, bodhicitta or right view. And if you're practicing tantra, it means keeping your mind in the tantric path. Awareness means being able to recognize when your mind is distracted, when your mind is not in Dharma. For example, when you meditate, remembrance is remembering the object of meditation and awareness is recognizing when your mind is distracted by another object. Perfect meditation has to be achieved with these two, remembrance and awareness. If you don't recognize that your mind has scattered from the object of meditation, you will waste many, many hours and then many days and then a lifetime. You will try to meditate but most of the time your mind will be too distracted by other objects. If you're trying to achieve calm abiding, you won't be able to achieve it. Even if you're just trying to keep your mind in virtue, in Dharma, you won't be able to do that.

PROTECTING YOUR MIND

Always protect the doors of your senses means that you close the doors of your senses to any object that causes attachment or any other negative emotional thought to arise. You protect yourself from seeing, hearing, smelling, tasting or touching those objects that cause attachment, anger and other negative emotional thoughts to arise.

The next part of the verse explains how to do that. You can protect yourself only if *three times day and night, again and again, you examine your mental continuum.* You have to examine your mind, your attitude to life. You have to watch what's happening in your mind all the time. If you don't watch, if you don't practice mindfulness, you can't tell whether your mind is Dharma or not Dharma, virtue or nonvirtue. It becomes dangerous, because of your negative thoughts. You then become an evil being, destroying yourself and also endangering and harming other sentient beings. This can happen if you don't examine your mind, if you don't practice mindfulness of what's happening in your mind.

December 31

Think, "The purpose of my life is to free all sentient beings from all their suffering and its causes and bring them to enlightenment. Therefore, I must achieve enlightenment. No matter how long it takes—how many lifetimes, how many eons—or how difficult it is, I'll do it; I'll work for enlightenment to liberate the numberless sentient beings from the oceans of samsaric suffering and bring them to enlightenment."

Yesterday we went over the verse from *The Bodhisattva's Jewel Garland* about always protecting the doors of the senses with remembrance, awareness and conscientiousness.

Kadampa Geshe Kharak Gomchung advises:

> When the desire to engage in an unrighteous activity arises, restrain your body and speech from moving toward that. If you do that, the benefits are that it eliminates the obstacles of both you and others and that you receive the common and supreme attainments.

Moving toward that means toward engaging in that unrighteous action.

There are one or two pages of advice from Kharak Gomchung, and every piece of advice ends with the expression *ang*—for example, *gom je ang*, which means *meditate on this*. There are about sixty *ang*s, and each *ang* is asking you to practice.[34]

You need to understand that if you restrain your body and speech from engaging in unrighteous actions you gain these special benefits, or advantages. Receiving the supreme attainment is the best

[34] We asked Geshe Thupten Jinpa about Geshe Kharak Gomchung's *ang*, and he replied: "I am aware of seventy *ang* by Kharak. This is a beautiful advice verse in seventy stanzas, each ending with the request term *ang*. (The *ang*s are preceded by not just one verb *gom*, but many other verbs.) There is in fact a reference to this in my *Mind Training: The Great Collection*. [See pp. 639–40, end of note 848: 'He is best known for his short poetic work entitled *Mind Training with Seventy Exhortations*....'] The full text is found in Thoyon Yeshe Dhondup's *Treasury of Gems* [pp. 257–64], but no English translation exists to my knowledge." For more about this lama, see *The Book of Kadam*, p. 661, note 547, for biographical information and pp. 601–608 for more of his sayings.

benefit that you get. It's very important to reflect on all the special advantages—in other words, profit— that you get because it encourages you and makes you happy to restrain your body and speech from unrighteous actions.

For example, the more we meditate, the more we discover how this body qualified by eight freedoms and ten endowments is precious and very meaningful and how we will have it almost only this one time because it will be difficult to find again. It is especially important to meditate on impermanence and death, the nature of life. It is not just that death itself can happen at any time but that what happens after that is related to karma. Even though we are trying to practice, in one day we collect more negative karma than good karma, because our mind is so uncontrolled that delusions pour down forcefully and uncontrollably, like a waterfall or a hailstorm. And we have created more negative karma than good karma not just in one day but throughout this life and throughout beginningless rebirths. Whether we will take rebirth in a lower or a higher realm, the body of a suffering or a happy transmigratory being, is defined by karma. It's up to karma; it's up to which karma we have collected more of. Unless we have purified our negative karma with perfect, powerful confession or by actualizing the path, if our death happened now, our rebirth would be in the lower realms with the most unbearable suffering and no freedom to practice Dharma.

THE SHORTCOMINGS OF SAMSARA

The more we reflect and meditate on these subjects, the more we feel that the whole of samsara is unbearable. Besides the desire realm, even the form and formless realms are only suffering in nature. The whole of samsara is only suffering in nature. The thought of having to reincarnate again in any of these realms is most disgusting, most terrifying, like jumping into a septic tank. You don't want to jump into a septic tank, where there are all those smelly, interesting things. You also don't want to jump into the center of a red-hot fire or into a nest of poisonous snakes. It would be terrifying to do that. You don't want that for even a moment. Because you know very clearly all the danger, unpleasantness and suffering you would experience, you don't have the slightest attraction to being in the middle of a septic tank, a fire or a nest of poisonous snakes.

This is true even for the deva realms within the desire, form and formless realms. In the desire realm there's the suffering of pain, the suffering of change (which means samsaric pleasures) and pervasive compounding suffering, aggregates under the control of karma and delusion. One meaning of *pervasive* is that the aggregates are the production of the impure cause, karma and delusion, and because of that, it is natural that they are pervaded by suffering. Also, because the aggregates are under the control of karma and delusion, they are suffering in nature. That's another meaning of *pervasive*. They are also contaminated by the seed of delusions, which is another meaning of *pervasive*. Because the seed of delusion is there, mental and physical problems can arise at any time from it. The seed compounds the suffering of this life and also produces delusion, which then produces karma, leaving a karmic seed on the continuity of the sixth consciousness, the mental consciousness; that karmic seed then produces the future rebirth, the future samsara.

These aggregates are pervasive compounding suffering, compounding the suffering of this life and the suffering of the future life by producing the future rebirth. This is the fundamental suffering of samsara. On the basis of these aggregates, we then experience the suffering of pain, all the sufferings to which even animals have aversion. Even animals don't want to suffer; they don't want to experience heat or cold or any other suffering of pain. Temporary samsaric pleasures, which come from pervasive compounding suffering, from these aggregates, are another suffering of samsara: the suffering of change. All three of these sufferings are experienced in the desire realm by humans and desire realm devas.

The devas of the form realm have no suffering of pain, but according to Geshe Sopa Rinpoche, they do have the suffering of change and, of course, pervasive compounding suffering. The aggregates of the devas in the form realm are under the control of karma and delusion and, of course, suffering in nature, and also contaminated by the seed of delusions.

The devas of the formless realm, though they don't have the other two sufferings, do have pervasive compounding suffering. That is the nature of their aggregates. Also, when their karma to be in the formless realm finishes, they have to reincarnate from there in the hell, hungry ghost, animal or some other realm.

We have been devas of the desire, form and formless realms numberless times in the past. Even those higher samsaric realms are not a new experience. However, all of those realms are disgusting. We human beings in the desire realm think that the sense pleasures of the desire realm are great and real happiness, because we can't see

that they are suffering in nature; but the beings of the form realm
see desire realm pleasures as totally disgusting and only suffering
in nature.

Through the six contemplations, or analyses, you move from
the desire realm to the form realm. With the first contemplation,
analysis of individual characteristics, you look at the desire realm as
only suffering in nature. You examine all the sense pleasures of the
human desire realm—sleep, sex, food and so forth—and discover
that they are only suffering in nature, as they *are* only suffering. You
then compare the desire realm to the form realm, where there is a
very long life with more peace and happiness. Through analysis you
discover that our realm, the human realm, and all human pleasures
are only suffering in nature. You look at the form realm as a better
realm, and your attachment then seeks that. However, you first have
to achieve *shamatha*, or calm abiding. That is the foundation. With
that as the preliminary, you then achieve the first of the four levels
of absorption.[35]

When you are born in the form realm, you see the desire realm
of human beings as disgusting. No matter how great we think our
pleasures are, those who are on the first level of absorption in the
form realm see them as completely disgusting. They don't have
any attraction to those pleasures for even a moment. All the pleasures that we think are so great, they see as only suffering. It's similar to the way we see disease and many other problems in our

[35] For further details see *Meditative States in Tibetan Buddhism; Opening the Eye of New
Awareness*, pp. 60–66, or *The Great Treatise on the Stages of the Path to Enlightenment*, Volume Three, pp. 96–103.

realm. When we think of Africa or some other place with a lot of contagious diseases and many people dying in epidemics and famines, we have no desire to be there for even a day—or even a minute. We're afraid of getting those diseases. This is how the beings in the form realm see even the human beings who have great wealth and pleasure. Here we're not talking about how they see arya beings or meditators who have entered the path and have renunciation of the whole of samsara. We're just talking about how the gods of the form realm see what we human beings believe to be great pleasure. They see it as totally disgusting and only so much suffering. They're not attracted to it at all.

The devas of the form realm go through all six contemplations. The second is contemplation arisen from belief. With the next, contemplation of isolation, they start to remove the gross delusions; they are actually removing the visible ones, not the imprints, or seeds. To remove imprints one needs the direct perception of emptiness and that, of course, depends on having renunciation of the whole of samsara, which devas of the form realm don't have.

After that, because they have removed the visible delusions, sometimes they feel happy and sometimes depressed. They then move though the contemplation of joy or withdrawal, during which they remove the three middling delusions. The fifth is contemplation of analysis. With the sixth, contemplation of final application, they remove the three subtle delusions. But these are all visible delusions.

It is by going through these six contemplations that you go from the desire realm to the form realm. From there, you go through the

four levels of absorption. When you are on the first level, you compare it to the second level and find that the second one is a better
state, with a longer life and more peace than the first. When you
analyze, you find that the first absorption has more suffering. You
then go through the six contemplations and reach the second
absorption. You again do analysis and find that the second absorption is suffering in nature and that the third absorption has more
peace and happiness. You then become attached to and seek the
third absorption. After completing the meditation through the six
contemplations, you then reach the third absorption. You then go
to the fourth absorption in a similar way.

You then become bored with even the inner happiness derived
from meditation and seek indifference. You then look at the form
realm as suffering in nature and see the formless realm as better.
Again you go through the meditation of the six contemplations.
After you have achieved the first level of the formless realm, limitless space, you again look at that state as only suffering in nature,
which *is* only suffering in nature, and look at the second level, limitless consciousness, as a better state. With attachment to the second level, you look at it as better and become totally detached from
the first one, limitless space. You then go through the meditation,
of the six contemplations and reach the second level, limitless consciousness. When you achieve that stage, you again look at it as only
suffering in nature and look at the next stage, nothingness, as better. You then seek that stage. You again go through the six contemplations, and achieve the third level, nothingness. When you have
reached that stage, you again look at it as suffering in nature and

look at the tip of samsara as better, as having more peace. You realize that compared to the tip of samsara, the state of nothingness is
only suffering in nature. Through the meditation of the six contemplations, you then achieve the tip of samsara.

Once you have achieved the tip of samsara, there's no higher
samsaric realm with which to compare it to discover that the tip of
samsara is only suffering in nature. There is no higher realm to find
better, more peaceful. Here you have total detachment to all desire
realm pleasures, seeing them as only suffering in nature. You see all
those pleasures as totally disgusting. The pleasures that we think are
great are hallucinations. You also see all the happiness of the form
realm as only suffering in nature; and you see even the first, second
and third levels of the formless realm as only suffering in nature.
The only thing that you don't discover is that the tip of samsara is
only suffering in nature. You don't discover that because there's no
higher realm with which to compare it. The problem is that you
have total renunciation of the desire realm, the form realm and the
first three levels of the formless realm, seeing everything except the
tip of samsara as only suffering in nature, but when that karma to
be in the tip of samsara finishes, you then have to be reborn again in
one of the lower samsaric realms. Sometimes a being believes that
they have achieved liberation when the many visible delusions are
removed. When their karma to be in the tip of samsara then finishes
and they see that they will have to be reborn again in one of those
realms, however, the heretical thought arises, "It's not true that there
is such a thing as liberation."

Here the important point you have to understand is that even though they had realized renunciation of the desire realm, the form realm and even the first three levels of the formless realm, feeling total aversion to them as disgusting, they again have to reincarnate because they didn't have renunciation of the tip of samsara, the last level of the formless realm. The point is that because they have no renunciation of that last level, they again reincarnate. Also, they don't have the wisdom that directly perceives emptiness. To stop reincarnating, you have to cease your delusions and the seeds of delusion, which are of the nature of imprints. To do that you need the wisdom that directly perceives emptiness. If you don't have that, you again have to reincarnate.

Thinking in this way can help some people to develop renunciation, or detachment.

You have to reflect on how the whole of samsara and all samsaric pleasures are only suffering in nature, as they *are* only suffering in nature. Like a scientist, you discover this through analytical meditation, and discovering their suffering nature encourages you to develop aversion to samsara and samsaric pleasures. You feel that samsara and samsaric pleasures are so disgusting that you wish to be free from all of them forever, particularly from those samsaric pleasures to which you have been strongly attached. Meditating on them, you discover that they are only suffering in nature. You also see the benefits of achieving the ultimate happiness of liberation, freedom forever from all suffering. Then, of course, there's also great liberation, or enlightenment. Discovering the suffering nature of samsara makes you very happy to restrain yourself from engaging in negative karma, in unrighteous actions. The more you meditate, the more you discover that samsara and samsaric pleasures are only suffering in nature, as they are only suffering in nature, and the more aversion to them you feel. Your wish to achieve liberation then becomes stronger.

You then take vows, either lay vows such as the eight precepts or five lay vows or ordination as a monk or nun, with thirty-six or 253 vows. You are very happy to take vows, and you are also very happy to live in those vows. You don't feel as if you living in a prison. The more analytical meditation you do, the more you discover the suffering nature of samsara and samsaric pleasures, especially the ones to which you are strongly attracted. The more you see that they are suffering, the more aversion to them you have and the stronger your wish to be free from them and achieve liberation. The very basic means to achieve liberation, to be free from this suffering, is by living in vows, either lay vows or the vows of a monk or nun. You are then very happy to do this, because you know that this is the path that protects you. This is your fundamental protection, protecting you from delusions, from negative karma and from all the sufferings of samsara.

The stronger your thought to achieve liberation, the happier your mind is when you're living in vows. It's not that anybody is forcing you; it comes from your own heart. It's as if you are suddenly being released after being in prison for a long time. On the day you're released you feel so happy. Like this, you feel so happy, day and night, knowing that living in vows is the way to get out of samsara. You're like somebody who has worked very hard all year and is now going on vacation. After working so hard, you now have

time to go skiing in the mountains or on the water. You're so happy
when you have a few days of vacation, but in this case, you're much
happier because you can attain the path and achieve liberation. You
can remove the cause of suffering, karma and delusion, and achieve
liberation forever. There's no coming back into suffering.

You need to think of all the shortcomings, all the harm and suffering for you and for others in this life and all the coming future
lives, if you engage in unrighteous actions with your body and
speech. You then think of all the benefits of eliminating your obstacles and those of others and of achieving the general and sublime
attainments.

This verse from Kharak Gomchung is similar to the third verse of
Eight Verses of Thought Transformation:

> In all conduct I will examine my own mental continuum.
> The moment a delusion arises, as it endangers me, mak-
> ing me and others evil, I will immediately practice force-
> fully averting it.

Take anger, for example. When you get angry, it also causes others to
get angry. Getting angry also destroys your merits. And by destroying your merits, you destroy not only your enlightenment, your liberation, the happiness of your future lives and your day-to-day peace
of mind, but those of others. When you get angry, you also cause
others to get upset and angry with you, which also destroys their
enlightenment, liberation, happiness of future lives and day-to-day
peace of mind. It endangers you, making you evil, and it also makes

others evil. Besides you, many other sentient beings are endangered. It creates obstacles to achieving liberation and enlightenment and creates negative karma, the cause to be reborn in the lower realms.

Whenever attachment or any other delusion arises, we have to avert it diligently and forcefully without even a second's delay. If you're even a second late, it will have already destroyed all your merits. In *A Guide to the Bodhisattva's Way of Life*, Shantideva says that if you get angry for one moment with a bodhisattva, who's a much higher being, you destroy the merits you have collected during one thousand eons by doing practices of charity, morality and so forth.[36] One moment of anger destroys all those things you did during a thousand eons. So, if you delay controlling your anger for even one moment, you are already defeated; you have already destroyed your merits and your liberation and enlightenment.

How are you going to forcefully avert the delusions without even a second's delay? By two means, method and wisdom. Applying the lam-rim meditations comes down to method and wisdom.

In general, without considering particular meditations, Kharak Gomchung talks here about restraining your body, speech and mind from engaging in unrighteous actions. He then talks about the benefits of doing that: you eliminate the obstacles of yourself and others. So, this is similar to the third stanza of *Eight Verses of Thought Transformation*, where it talks about what makes you and others evil. Kharak Gomchung talks here about eliminating the obstacles of yourself and others. If you are controlled by delusion and then

---

[36] Ch. 6, v. 1

engage in negative karma, you also cause others to generate delusion and engage in negative karma. That's the main obstacle.

Kharak Gomchung then says that you achieve the common and sublime attainments. The common attainments are the eight siddhis.[37] The sublime attainment, or siddhi, is enlightenment. Here, what gives you encouragement is thinking of these shortcomings of not restraining your body, speech and mind from engaging in unrighteous actions and of the benefits of doing so. That's extremely important.

CONTROLLING DELUSIONS

Since it's a very important subject, I would like to elaborate a little on the third stanza of *The Eight Verses* and the lines from *The Bodhisattva's Jewel Garland*, *Three times day and night, again and again, examine your mental continuum.*

When there's danger that a delusion will arise, you have to apply meditation to control it. If you don't defeat your attachment, anger and other delusions, if you always give the victory to your delusions and take the loss on yourself—in other words, if you don't practice Dharma—what happens now and in the future is that your delusions increase, becoming more difficult to control. It says in a sutra that for those who are attached to sleep, their sleep becomes heavier and deeper, and their life then becomes very difficult. It is the same

[37] The eight siddhis are: magical sword, magical pills, magical eye medicine giving power to see objects at great distances, the power of miraculous walking, the magical elixir of youth, miraculously changing the physical form, the power to vanish miraculously, the power to pass through material barriers.

for those who have great attachment to alcohol. It makes them drink more and more, which then creates many difficulties and destroys their life. They're even unable to do their job, and it brings many other problems.

If you always allow delusion to arise, giving the victory to delusion and taking the loss on yourself, if you always allow yourself to be controlled by delusion, if you allow a tsunami of delusion to arise in your mind, you leave many negative imprints on your mental continuum. Each time attachment arises, it leaves a negative imprint on your mental continuum, so the imprint then becomes deeper and deeper. If you don't practice patience, each time anger arises, it leaves a negative imprint on your mental continuum, so the negative imprint becomes deeper and deeper. That makes your future lives very difficult. It makes it very difficult for you to practice Dharma, to avert or abandon delusions. It is similar with pride and any other delusion. It makes the future very difficult, because the deeper the negative imprint, the more difficult it will be for you to control your delusions.

Negative imprints are much more terrifying than the sufferings of hell. With hell suffering, you experience it, then when the karma to be in hell is exhausted, the suffering stops. However, negative imprints make delusions arise again and again. If you leave a negative imprint, delusion will uncontrollably arise from that imprint again and again. Even though you might know the meditation techniques very well and be able to explain them, if you're unable to practice them when delusion arises, your life then becomes very uncontrolled. Your life is controlled by delusion, and you then uncontrollably engage in negative karma. Therefore, you need to think of negative imprints when you're in danger of giving rise to strong delusion in your daily life. It's not an easy or simple thing to control delusion, but it's so harmful if a delusion leaves a negative imprint on your mind, as it makes your life difficult now and in the future, causing you to engage again and again in heavy negative karmas.

It's very important to remember what is said in the sutra *A Hundred Karmas*, which describes what happens if we don't control our mind and we engage in negative karma. This is very important to understand and to write down in your notebooks, daily prayer book or diary.

> Each time you engage in negative karma, it makes you habituated to nonvirtue.

You become habituated to nonvirtue, like someone addicted to drugs or alcohol. Normally the Tibetan expression that I've translated as *habituated* means to become familiar with something, but here it may have a slightly different meaning. I think it means that you become accustomed to being uncontrolled.

> What happens not only now but in the future (of this life and after this life) is that you again depend on nonvirtuous activities. In the future (of this life and after this life), you again engage in the same negative karma. By following negative karma, you get reborn again and again.

This is similar to the verse in *The Foundation of All Good Qualities* where it talks about how your rebirth follows negative karma like a shadow follows a body.[38] You get reborn again and again because you follow negative karma.

It's very important to remember this quotation from Buddha's teaching, from this sutra *A Hundred Karmas*, when you're in danger of giving rise to delusion and engaging in negative karma in your daily life. Remember that this is something that goes on and on, not only in this life but in future lives. It makes things very difficult for you. You continuously engage in negative karma and continuously reincarnate and endlessly experience suffering, particularly the sufferings of the lower realms and of the human realm. When you think of Buddha's explanation of the dangers, you don't want to engage in negative karma for even a second. You immediately want to stop engaging in negative karma. You don't want to imprison yourself in suffering in all your future lives.

If you attempt to abandon or reduce your delusions when they're about to arise or are arising, you also leave less imprint on your mental continuum. The negative imprint, the cause of delusions, becomes thinner and thinner.

I'm going to mention here five points on how to control the mind from *A Guide to the Bodhisattva's Way of Life*. The first point is that if you follow delusion and don't practice Dharma, don't rely on the teachings, since your delusions become heavier and heavier, the

[38] After death, just like a shadow follows the body
 The results of black and white karma follow.

negative imprints become deeper and deeper, making your life very difficult now and in the future. Remembering this is the first technique to control your mind so that you stop engaging in negative karma.

The second technique is to look at delusion as your enemy. You then generate the remedy to delusion. To look at delusion as your enemy is essential. If you look at anger as a friend (or, as His Holiness the Dalai Lama says, as somebody who is behind you, supporting and protecting you) and not as your enemy, it will harm and destroy you and others. This is similar to what I mentioned before about the quotations from *The Eight Verses* and Kharak Gomchung. And it is the same with attachment.

A most important thing in daily life is to look at delusion as your enemy or as a mental sickness, a chronic disease of the mind. You have to recognize it as a sickness, as something you have to remove or renounce. If you had cancer, you would look for any method in the world that could remove it. It is similar here. The delusions are terrifying. If you understand the unbelievable harm that delusion causes you, you will look at it as your enemy, and the courage will then come to apply its remedy. You will stop following delusion and be able to defeat, or eliminate, it. This is how to look at delusions as your enemy and make yourself powerful.

I remember once giving some advice to a Sangha member in relation to doing retreat or living in their vows. I don't remember everything I said to them, but I was comparing their situation to the war in Iraq. (It doesn't apply just to the war in Iraq but to any war.) In a war you're killing other sentient beings, who are actually the most precious beings from whom you receive all your past, present and future happiness, liberation and enlightenment. You're killing all those precious beings from whom you receive all your happiness. However, what you're doing by living in your vows is making war on your delusions instead of on Iraq. To live in your vows, you meditate on making war on your delusions, on defeating the enemy that harms you and other sentient beings from life to life. You think of how your delusions directly or indirectly harm all sentient beings from life to life. Making war to defeat your delusions is the real war, the most important war, and the real hero is the one who defeats their delusions. A war hero is a false hero, because they kill the sentient beings from whom they receive all their past, present and future happiness.

Here Shantideva says:

> Even if I am burned, even if my head is cut off, even if I am killed, I will never surrender to my enemy, the delusions.[39]

That's to give yourself courage.

The next point is that an external enemy doesn't harm you all the time, from life to life, but delusion does. Your inner enemy, delusion, has harmed you during beginningless rebirths up to now, it is harming you now, and it will continuously harm you in the future if you don't eliminate it. It harms you all the time, in all lifetimes.

[39] Ch. 7, v. 62

Think, "My enemy, delusion, has no beginning and no end. No other enemies become my enemy for such a long time. No external enemy harms me in all lifetimes." By thinking this, you see that any external enemy is insignificant and that it is delusion that is your real enemy. Thinking in this way encourages you to do something to defeat delusion. You don't want to allow delusion to arise, or if it arises, you want to do something to eliminate it. That's the second part of the second point.

The third point is that if you take the side of an external enemy, that enemy will stop harming you and will even help you; but the more you become the friend of delusion, the closer you become to delusion, the more powerful and dangerous it becomes.

Here Shantideva says:

If you help your external enemy, it makes them happy.
But the more you become friends with delusion, the more
it harms you.[40]

Helping an external enemy brings peace and happiness to everyone, to both you and the people around you. But if you take the side of delusion, if you become friends with delusion, delusion then becomes more powerful and makes you suffer more and more.

The following story is an example of this. Quite a number of years ago at a dinner party in Sydney, a student was talking about how his next-door neighbor, who was unhappy or jealous, had scratched his

[40] Ch. 4, v. 33

new car. The student didn't know what to do about it. George Farley, who was an FPMT board member at that time, said, "If it was Lama Zopa, he would give him a present." I don't know how he came up with this idea.

The family whose car had been scratched then tried to think of a present they could give to their neighbor. When they checked, they found that he liked golf, so they bought him some expensive golf balls. When they went to his house and gave him the golf balls, he seemed very happy, though I don't think he said much at that time. That same day or the next day, however, he came to their house and told them that he appreciated what they had done very much. Because he was happy, the family was happy. Everyone was happy.

This accords exactly with what Shantideva says: if you become harmonious with an external enemy and help them, it brings peace and happiness to everyone. That's exactly right. But it is the total opposite with delusions. The more you are in harmony with delusions, the more harmful they become. So, that's another meditation to encourage you to overcome delusion.

The fourth point in overcoming delusions is to remember that an external enemy harms just your belongings, your body or your life. Even if your enemy kills you, he is just separating your consciousness from this body—nothing more than that. That's the worst harm he can do to you. But if you follow delusion, if you take the side of delusion, delusion makes you to be continuously reborn in samsara and to experience the unimaginable oceans of samsaric suffering.

Here Shantideva says:

Even if the asuras, suras and all the other sentient beings
of the six realms become your enemy, they cannot lead
you down into the fires of the Inexhaustible Hell.[41]

Inexhaustible Hell—the eighth, or lowest, hot hell realm—has the
heaviest suffering of all of the lower realms, of all of samsara, and
the longest duration of life, one intermediate eon. Delusion destroys
whatever it encounters. Your powerful enemy, delusion, brings
you to the lower realms, even to the Inexhaustible Hell, where you
experience unimaginable suffering. The fires of Inexhaustible Hell
could burn even the great mountain, Mount Meru, into dust in one
second.[42]

Even if nobody kills you, following delusion makes you engage in
negative karma, which then brings you into the lower realms, into
the hell realms. But if you haven't collected negative karma, even if
another sentient being kills you, since you don't have the cause to
be born in the lower realms, negative karma, you won't go to the
lower realms.

In regard to an external enemy, people think, "Oh, my enemy is
so harmful! One day he insulted me and another day he glared at
me." You can tell a lot of stories about how someone has harmed
you, and each one becomes a reason to prove that person is bad.
Here you should tell similar stories about your inner enemy, the
delusions.

These meditation techniques help you to see delusion as your

[41] Ch. 4, v. 30
[42] See ch. 4, v. 31

enemy, so that you become strong and have the courage not to follow and to defeat delusion. If you're living in vows, doing retreat or practicing Dharma, what you hear all the time is that you need to be strong. You need to be strong because if you're weak, delusion will overpower you and then you can't practice Dharma; you can't achieve liberation or enlightenment, nor even the happiness of future lives. Since you can't have even day-to-day peace of mind, you can't help others. Here with all these words Shantideva is inspiring you to have courage and to be strong. That's very important to remember in your daily life. You need to make yourself very strong, stronger than delusion, so that you can defeat delusion, giving the victory to yourself and the loss to delusion. You need to do that so that delusion doesn't get to leave more and more negative imprints on your mind, which then make your future lives very difficult.

The fifth point is that you have to make yourself strong and have courage so that you're able to defeat delusion. With an external enemy, even if you kick them out of an area or a country, they will later come back to harm you. But once you have removed this inner enemy, it's impossible for it to arise again.[43] Like a seed that is burned and cannot grow again, once you've defeated the inner enemy, delusion, it's impossible for it to come back again.

Thinking in the different ways mentioned here gives you the courage and inspiration to abandon delusion. Later, without the obstacle of delusion, you'll gradually be able to actualize the path to enlightenment, and you'll then be able to remove even the cause

[43] See ch. 4, v. 45

of delusion, the negative imprint, making it impossible for delusion to arise again.

REMEMBERING IMPERMANENCE AND DEATH

Another technique to control delusion is to meditate on teachings on impermanence and death. There are some important analyses by Gungtang Rinpoche, a very high Amdo lama. I met the incarnation of Gungtang Rinpoche, a great lama from Amdo who has been preserving Lama Tsongkhapa's teachings purely, at a World Buddhist Fellowship conference in Nepal. His Holiness Panchen Rinpoche was brought to Nepal for the conference by the Chinese government, and Rinpoche was always surrounded by many Chinese government officials. During the conference, Rinpoche stood up and said just a few words: "May the activities of the Triple Gem spread in all ten directions." At the time I thought the words might be related to His Holiness the Dalai Lama's activities spreading all over the world.

At a World Buddhist Fellowship function to welcome the king of Nepal, the Theravadin monks wanted the Tibetan lamas to move down, because they didn't want the Tibetan lamas to be ahead of them. Gungtang Rinpoche didn't move; he just stayed where he was. It's just a memory I have of Gungtang Rinpoche.

I also saw Gungtang Rinpoche in Tibet at Tashi Kyil, the largest monastery in Amdo. It's a huge monastery where many thousands of monks are engaged in excellent study. The second time I went on pilgrimage in Tibet, I went to Tashi Kyil and saw Gungtang

Rinpoche. Rinpoche said that the main temple of the monastery had been burnt down by the Chinese but the teaching of Buddha had not been destroyed. Twenty years before there were no monks as they had been tortured or killed and nothing was happening in the monastery. But after Mao Zedong died and Deng Xiaoping took over, all the great masters and scholars who had survived were able to come back to the monastery and educate the young monks. Rinpoche said sixty or seventy great scholars there were expert in sutra and about twenty of them were also expert in tantra. Tashi Kyil is an unbelievably inspiring monastery.

I think these teachings on impermanence and death come from the previous incarnation of Gungtang Rinpoche. The following instruction is very important.

> The evil friend, the friend of negative karma, isn't some-
> body who has horns growing on his head. The evil friend
> is someone who acts as if he really loves you, like a mother
> loves her beloved child. The child who knows that their
> mother (or father) is so kind holds them most dear.

The evil friend, the friend of negative karma, doesn't come to you with horns on his head or in some other fearful form. He smiles at you and acts as if he loves you very much. He becomes your friend and, loving and laughing, supports you in engaging in various distractions, in various actions that are opposite to conscientiousness. By being your friend, he distracts you and makes you engage in actions of non-conscientiousness. (I've probably just made a new

English word!) So, that is the friend of negative karma. Like a contagious disease, his influence gradually spreads out.

> Abandon that nonvirtuous friend, who is like a smiling
> cannibal or the *hala* plant.

The cannibal's intention is to eat you, but in order to get you, he smiles at you and acts as if he loves you; when you know that, you don't follow him, you abandon him. It is the same with the hala plant. By knowing it's a poisonous plant, you abandon it.

You should write down this advice from Gungtang Rinpoche in your notebook or your daily prayer book as a reminder, so that you don't get cheated, or deceived. You're then able to protect yourself and continue to practice Dharma. Without obstacles you're then able to protect your vows and attain realizations. A lot of obstacles happen if you're unable to understand what Gungtang Rinpoche has explained.

It's also helpful to think in the way that Kharak Gomchung explains:

> At present we have a choice between the happiness of the
> upper realms and the sufferings of the evil-gone realms.
> Reflect on this.

At the moment you can choose between the happiness beyond this life up to enlightenment and the sufferings of the three lower realms. You should reflect on these two things together.

You have a choice. Do you want to achieve the happiness beyond this life up to enlightenment or do you want to have the sufferings of the lower realms? Every day you have the choice of which one to take, of which way to think. If you want the happiness beyond this life up to enlightenment, today you should engage in practicing Dharma; your body, speech and mind should live in Dharma, in lam-rim, and especially in bodhicitta. You should practice the three principal aspects of the path and, on top of that, tantra (if you're qualified to practice tantra). In one day, one hour, one minute and even one second, you have a choice between the sufferings of the lower realms and the happiness of future lives. Even in each second, you have a choice between hell and enlightenment, between samsara and nirvana. As I mentioned yesterday, happiness and suffering are up to how we think. If what you want is not hell but enlightenment, you need to keep your mind in bodhicitta. If you want to achieve liberation from samsara, if you want to achieve realizations, if you want to achieve the happiness of future lives, engage in the lam-rim path. If you generate bodhicitta, you achieve all those kinds of happiness: the happiness of future lives, liberation from samsara and enlightenment.

When you're in a situation where you are about to give rise to delusion or engage in heavy negative karma, immediately remember this advice and ask yourself, "What do I want?" You then realize that you have a choice. It reminds you that if you abandon delusion and negative karma, you then achieve the happiness of future lives, liberation and enlightenment. You will then keep your mind in the path.

It is also helpful to think, "If I choose these few moments of pleasure, I give up the ultimate happiness of liberation and enlightenment. Will I choose this small, short-term pleasure and sacrifice all
this? Or will I give up this small pleasure to achieve liberation and
enlightenment?" If you renounce those few moments of pleasure,
you get all the ultimate happiness of liberation and enlightenment.
But if you seek those few moments of temporary pleasure, you then
lose liberation and enlightenment. This is also a useful way to overcome delusion.

In *Good Explanation* Sakya Pandita advises:

> One who is attached to small pleasure will not achieve the
> great happiness.

If you are attached to small, short-term samsaric pleasures, you
won't achieve the great happiness, which means not only the happiness of all your coming future lives but especially liberation and
enlightenment.

It also means that someone who is attached to sleep, food and
other short-term pleasures can't bear hardships to practice Dharma.
This is someone who can't bear the hardships to achieve liberation and enlightenment and to enlighten all sentient beings. This
is someone who can't achieve all those great successes. Someone who's attached to small, short-term pleasures can't bear hardships to practice Dharma for the long-term happiness of all the
coming future lives, liberation and enlightenment, and then being
able to enlighten all sentient beings. This advice is also helpful in

overcoming delusions. It encourages you to become powerful in destroying your enemy, delusion.

Also, Kadampa Geshe Kharak Gomchung gave the following advice, which is based on a verse in *A Guide to the Bodhisattva's Way of Life*.

> By depending on the human boat,
> You cross the great river of suffering.
> Since this boat will be difficult to find again,
> While you have it, don't be lazy.

This verse shows what you can do with this human body that you have received: you can cross the oceans of samsaric suffering, you can be liberated from the oceans of samsaric suffering. Since you have such a body almost only one time and it will be difficult to find again, don't get distracted. Rather than getting attached to small pleasures, look to achieve great happiness.

Also, as *A Guide to the Bodhisattva's Way of Life* says:

> It's not certain which will come first—tomorrow or the next life. Therefore, rather than working for tomorrow, it is better to work for the next life.

These pieces of great advice remind us of impermanence and death. Tomorrow is uncertain, but our next life will definitely happen, and it could happen at any time. Therefore, we should work for the happiness of that future life. This is why it's so important to practice Dharma.

A Guide to the Bodhisattva's Way of Life also says:

> You can't just relax, saying "I'm not going to die today."

If you truthfully and deeply question yourself, you can't sign a guarantee that you're not going to die today. You can't really see what is going to happen to you, not even in the next hour or the next minute. It's totally dark. Since you can't see what's going to happen, how could you guarantee that you're not going to die today?

The thought that you're going to live for a long time continues even to the day of your death. This thought that you're going to live for many years is there that same morning of (and even immediately before) the accident or heart attack that kills you. It's not true, and it cheats you.

These pieces of advice on different ways to think about impermanence and death encourage you so that you are then able to defeat delusion, thus ending your samsara and your suffering. The continuation of your suffering has no beginning, but now you can end it. Of course, your ultimate aim is to achieve enlightenment for sentient beings, but at least here you end your own suffering of samsara.

THE BODHISATTVA'S JEWEL GARLAND

I will now give the oral transmission of *The Bodhisattva's Jewel Garland* by quickly reading the English translation, which will become the oral transmission; and if you understand the meaning, you then receive the commentary as well. If the English translation is correct, you can do an oral transmission in English. But if it's not correct, it's better to read the Tibetan; otherwise, you will miss some words and other words will be incorrect.

The Jewel Rosary of the Practice of Bodhicitta

I bow down to great compassion,
To all my spiritual masters,
And to my deities of devotion.

Having cast away all my doubts
About the value of spiritual practice,
I shall exert myself in the practice
Of the bodhisattva path.

Having removed sleepiness, dullness and laziness,
I shall always be joyful
When engaging in such incredible practices.

I shall guard the doors of my speech, body and mind
Against any negative action,
By constantly being alert and mindful in my behavior.

This word *alert* is quite often used in the United States. After bin Laden, this word *alert* has been announced many times; but I don't think they're announcing an alert against the real enemy, delusions and negative karma.

Since the Tibetan here is *dren pa she shin bag yö*, you have to have all three terms in the English. *Alert* is fine for *bag yö*, conscientiousness, but *dren pa she shin* means remembrance and awareness. These are two things that you need when you do the practice of calm abiding. Because each one has a particular function, I think all three terms need to be translated separately.

> I shall examine my mind
> Over and over again, day and night.

> I proclaim my faults, not seeking faults in others,
> Hide my own good qualities but praise those of others.

Even though it's difficult to do this, we have to try, even if it's only once or twice a day. If we try to do it one time, we will succeed one time, and we will then succeed two times, three times....

> Not seeking material gain or veneration from others,
> I will be able to abandon any desire for fame,
> Being content with whatever I have.
> I shall not fail to repay
> Whatever kindness I receive from others
> And shall meditate on love and compassion,
> Reminding myself always of bodhicitta,
> The altruistic mind of enlightenment.

> I abandon the ten nonvirtuous actions
> And consolidate my faith in spiritual practice.

Having abandoned pride over my qualities
And disdain towards others,
Always humble,
I abandon wrong livelihood and follow right livelihood.

Having given up all meaningless activity,
I shall be endowed
With the inner jewel of arya beings.

Having given up all meaningless activity,
I remain in solitude,
Abandon senseless talk
And discipline my speech.

Whenever I see my spiritual master
I pay respect from my heart,
And with equal respect
Hold even ordinary sentient beings to be my great teachers,
As I hold great arya beings to be.

Quite a number of years ago when I was in Melbourne, Australia, Samdup Tsering, a Tibetan who was Geshe Doga's translator for many years, told me an interesting story. Samdup had found a job in a Japanese shop, and he told me that everybody in the shop was instructed by their boss that they must regard every customer as someone very precious and be very kind to them. That's very interesting. Of course, it wasn't done for the happiness of other sentient beings; I think it was a policy to enable the shop to successfully sell things and make money. I can't say what the boss's motivation was, but it may have been self-centered. The attitude was like that, and the external method was to show kindness.

Of course, here in Dharma, in Tibetan Mahayana Buddhism, being kind is not for your own happiness but for the happiness of other sentient beings. The main aim is to bring happiness to other sentient beings. You think that others are precious and you then respect and are kind to them. With your mind you think that they're precious and kind, and with your body and speech you help them. You talk to them respectfully and respect them with the actions of your body. You do that not for your happiness but for theirs. Your kindness is sincere, not political. With political kindness, you are actually doing things for yourself with a self-centered attitude but acting as if you care for others. Your kindness is just a show.

I think this boss was very smart and taught the people who worked for him an interesting technique. However, I think you should practice cherishing others as it's described here in *The Bodhisattva's Jewel Garland* or in the practices of Mahayana Buddhism.

Nagarjuna explained that there are two attitudes you should have in daily life, not only for your own happiness but for the happiness of all the numberless sentient beings. The first attitude you should have is, "This person (or animal) is my wish-granting jewel. I receive from them all my numberless past, present and future happiness, liberation and enlightenment. They are most precious and most kind."

After you have discovered that they are most precious, Nagarjuna explains that you then think, "I myself am like a wish-granting jewel, fulfilling all the wishes of sentient beings." In essence, you first think that each sentient being is the most precious one, a wish-fulfilling jewel that is fulfilling all your wishes for happiness up to enlightenment. You then think that you yourself become like a wish-fulfilling jewel, fulfilling all that sentient being's wishes for happiness.

You can also think that you become like a wish-granting tree, fulfilling all wishes. In a pure land, when you pray to a wish-granting tree, everything you pray for is materialized. It fulfills all your wishes.

You think, "May I myself become like a wish-granting jewel, fulfilling all sentient beings' desires. And may I become like a wish-granting tree that fulfills all their wishes." You yourself become like a wish-granting jewel and a wish-granting tree for sentient beings, fulfilling all their wishes for happiness.

First think of the other being, who is so kind and precious, as a wish-fulfilling jewel from whom you receive all your happiness of the three times. Next, think that you yourself become like a wish-granting jewel and a wish-granting tree, fulfilling all that sentient being's wishes for happiness.

Even if you are living alone, this is what you should practice; and this is what you should especially practice when you're dealing with people, whether you're working in a school, an office, a family home or a Dharma center. This attitude should be there as much as possible in your daily life. When you remember how each sentient being is most precious and most kind, you naturally respect them, and you talk very nicely, very kindly, to them. Your heart cherishes that being the most, and the way you behave toward them is respectful.

You become very kind and would do anything to help that person or animal.

Here I'd like to mention another point. Whatever help, however small, you give an animal or person with this good heart is an offering to all the buddhas. It's the best offering to all the buddhas and bodhisattvas. Even if you give only some small comfort or pleasure to that sentient being, whether human or non-human, it's the offering most pleasing to all the buddhas and bodhisattvas. Why? Because this sentient being, even if it's an insect, is what the numberless buddhas and bodhisattvas cherish the most; this is what they hold in their hearts. Like a mother cherishes her beloved child most in her heart, this sentient being, even if it's a mosquito or some other bug, is cherished most by all the numberless buddhas and bodhisattvas. This insect, this beggar or this person who is angry with you and abuses you is cherished like their heart by the numberless bodhisattvas. Day and night the numberless bodhisattvas pray for this being. They work, dedicate their merits and try to achieve all the realizations, including enlightenment, for this sentient being.

The numberless buddhas achieved enlightenment for whom? For sentient beings, for this person, for this insect. Guru Shakyamuni Buddha collected merits for three countless great eons for this sentient being; Buddha achieved enlightenment for this sentient being. He sacrificed everything—his wealth when born as a king, his body and his life—for this sentient being. He sacrificed himself numberless times during countless great eons to make charity and practice the rest of the six paramitas for this sentient being. He achieved enlightenment for this sentient being. Buddha is working for all sentient beings, and that includes this sentient being. So, this sentient being is what is cherished most by Guru Shakyamuni Buddha and the rest of the numberless buddhas.

Therefore, even though you might offer just a little help for a small problem, it's the best offering to the numberless buddhas and bodhisattvas. It's the offering most pleasing to them. It is like saying a few words of praise to a beloved child; even those few nice words to her child make the mother very happy. And if you criticize or say a few nasty words to that child, it makes the mother very upset.

Buddha said in the *Avatamsaka Sutra*:

> Any harm to a sentient being is a great harm to me. Any benefit to a sentient being is a supreme benefit to me. I and sentient beings are equal in happiness and suffering. And I have achieved the rupakaya for the benefit of sentient beings.

It is very important to remember this in daily life. It is also helpful to remember that anything you do to sentient beings affects the numberless buddhas and bodhisattvas, the ones to whom you pray to receive blessings to actualize the path, the ones you are trying to become. When you remember that, you naturally do everything you can, great or small, to help sentient beings. You treat every sentient being, every human being and even every insect, in the best way.

You must do this practice, especially if you're working or dealing with people in everyday life but even if you're living alone and not working in any organization. You must remember to do this practice. This is a key practice, especially in a Dharma organization. Working in a Dharma center means being kind to everybody. You don't have to be rude. It's not that you can give everybody what they need. You can't perform magic and give a billion dollars to everybody. However, even if you can give only limited help, at least the way you behave and the way you talk to people should be very respectful and very kind. You shouldn't get upset with people, and other people will see and appreciate that. Even if you can't help someone, the way you explain that you can't help them should at least be respectful.

You have to do this because you're working in what's called a Dharma center, a meditation center. Meditation means training the mind; meditation means taming, or subduing, the mind. Of course a Dharma center is totally different from an ordinary company, which isn't based on Dharma teachings. As I explained in relation to the manager of the Japanese shop, even though the motivation might be selfish and not sincere, it's still good externally to be respectful and kind. That's essential.

If you can do something to help someone, you do it. Of course, as an ordinary being, you don't have psychic powers so you can't give people everything that they need; but you should do whatever you can. However, if you can't help them, at least you shouldn't be rude to them. You should be kind and respectful, and with your mind you should cherish that person. As Nagarjuna advises, you should cherish that sentient being as most precious and most kind. If that is your attitude, the way you communicate will naturally be respectful and kind. A Dharma center is very different from a company or business, which is based on money. You pay someone money and if they don't do their job properly, you kick them out. It's simple, because you pay them. A Dharma organization is very different from that.

Also, a Dharma organization has to set an example. It should be an inspiration to others to practice Dharma, to practice the good heart. Whether you're an old student or a new student who doesn't know much about Dharma, you should be an inspiring example so that people see the signs of Tibetan Mahayana Buddhist practice. This is very important.

> Whenever I meet others
> I regard older ones as my parents,
> Those of similar age or younger
> As my brother, sister or relative.

> Having abandoned bad influence from others,
> I shall follow spiritual friends,
> Be happy myself wherever I go,
> Without any ill will towards others,
> And not be discontented with my life.

> I abandon attachment to any desirable things
> And remain desireless,
> For attachment in any form
> Can never lead to a happy rebirth.

Instead, it takes away the life-force

Of liberation from suffering.

I shall exert myself in any virtuous activity

That can lead me to ultimate happiness,

Accomplishing first whatever practices I have started.

Thus, I will be able to accomplish all my practices,

Otherwise none of my tasks will be accomplished.

I take no interest in those activities

That can be harmful to others,

And cast away pride over my qualities

Whenever it arises in my mind.

I must remind myself always

Of the instructions of my spiritual teacher.

I shall be able to encourage myself

Whenever I feel depressed,

Whenever my mind is deluded by attachment to myself

And hatred towards others,

I shall be able to realize that both I and others

Are equally void of inherent existence,

And view myself and others

As being illusory-like, a magic form.

Whenever I hear unpleasant words,

I view them as echoes.

Whenever my body is harmed by others,

I shall be able to view it as being
The result of my previous negative karma.

Abiding always in solitude,
Like the corpse of a wild animal,
I shall keep myself away from the temptation
Of meaningless activities,
And remain desireless,
Reminding myself always of my deity of devotion.

Whenever laziness or laxity arise in my mind,
I shall be able to remove them immediately
And always remember the essence of moral behavior.

Whenever I meet others,
Having removed angry behavior,
I shall be able to speak sincerely and frankly,
With a smiling face.

This *smiling face* is not a political, or diplomatic, smiling face. Sometimes, because you can't really smile, you just move the corners of your mouth up, but it doesn't look nice. You know that it's not natural, and it doesn't make you happy. The smile here is not a political smile, but a smile that comes from the good heart. The purpose of smiling is not for your happiness, but for the happiness of other people. If your smile is for that, it is then Dharma, pure Dharma. Showing a gentle, smiling face to others out of the good heart makes other sentient beings happy. The smile is not to make you happy but to make others happy. Your smiling to make other sentient beings happy causes you to have a beautiful body in future lives. That's the temporary benefit.

Whenever I meet others,
I shall not be jealous of them,
But be generous to them.
I abandon any dispute with others
And concern myself with their welfare and comfort.

I shall not be fickle in any relationships with others,
But remain firm.
I give up any form of humiliating others
And always respect them.

Whenever I give advice to others,
I shall do so with sincerity and sympathy.
I abandon any disrespect for other forms of spiritual practice
And appreciate whatever religions others are interested in.
I shall be able to remain with the practice of the ten virtues,
    day and night.
I shall dedicate whatever virtues I have done in the past,
Do now and will do in the future,
To the benefit of other sentient beings.

Through performing the seven-limb prayer
I pray for the happiness of all other beings.

Thus I will be able to accomplish

The merit of wisdom and skillful means,

And will be able to eliminate all delusions,

For in this way,

I shall be able to attain enlightenment

For the sake of all sentient beings.

Thus I will be able to achieve great meaning

From finding this precious human rebirth.

There are seven gems that adorn the minds

   of bodhisattvas:

The gem of faith,

The gem of instruction,

The gem of contemplation,

The gem of wisdom,

The gem of ethics,

The gem of modesty,

And the gem of generosity.

These seven gems have limitless virtuous qualities.

When I practice these inner gems within myself,

I should not reveal any to those

Who are not yet mature to practice these excellent qualities.

I shall be heedful of my speech

In the presence of others,

And be heedful of my thoughts

In isolation from others.

This translation of *The Bodhisattva's Jewel Garland* is by Geshe Nam-gyal Wangchen, a great scholar and teacher in Drepung Loseling monastery, who is educating His Holiness Ling Rinpoche's incarnation and quite a few other incarnations who in their past lives were outstanding scholars in the largest monasteries in Tibet. He was the resident teacher in Jamyang Buddhist Centre, our London center, for many years. I think he was there seven years or even longer. He was alone there. There were no other Sangha living in this big city of London, where there's an explosion of delusions—or the advertising of delusions, anyway. He lived for many years in this big city of London, totally alone.

Kadampa Teachings 4

BODHGAYA, DECEMBER 2007

Geshe Chekawa (1101–75)

Jerry Powers

··· Kadampa Teachings 4 ···

December 27

THERE ARE MANY Kadampa teachings. *Mind Training: The Great Collection* is a collection of about fifty teachings and instructions from various Kadampa lamas, which Geshe Thupten Jinpa, His Holiness the Dalai Lama's translator, has translated into English.[44] The text I have here, *The Heart Advice of the Kadam Teachings: A Fine Vase of Nectar*, was actually composed by Kachen Yeshe Gyaltsen, but it is regarded as a Kadampa teaching. It is a Kadampa teaching.[45]

I requested the previous Root Institute directors to obtain statues of some of the Kadampa geshes. You don't normally see these holy objects. It's a little more common to see statues of Lama Atisha, but not so common to see statues of the others. My idea was to give some teachings on different Kadampa texts. That was my motivation, anyway, though it could just be an ego trip.

At this time, I thought to give just the oral transmission of this text by Kachen Yeshe Gyaltsen, as I recently received the oral transmission of almost all the teachings composed by this great lama at

[44] Since Rinpoche gave this teaching Geshe Jinpa has also published *The Book of Kadam*, a collection of texts closely associated with Atisha and Dromtönpa.
[45] See *The Book of Kadam*, pp. 529–58, or appendix 4 of this book for a translation of the first chapter.

Lama Ösel's house at Sera Monastery in south India. Quite a number of other monks attended, including some incarnate lamas and ex-abbots, including the ex-abbots of Tashi Lhunpo Monastery, the Panchen Lama's monastery, and of the Tantric College. I missed about three days of the teachings when I had to go to Bombay because we had invited His Holiness the Dalai Lama there to give teachings to the Indian people.

However, in New York I recently received the teachings I had missed from Khyongla Rato Rinpoche, an elderly lama who became a geshe in Tibet but later took the lay aspect. He has lived in New York for many years. Rinpoche is a great treasury of lineages, holding the lineage of the entire teaching of Buddha, the *Kangyur*, and the *Tengyur*, as well as lineages of the collections of teachings and commentaries of all the pandits, or great scholars. Rinpoche has received the oral transmission of the *Kangyur* two times, first from his teacher at the place where he was born and the second time from, I think, Pari Dorje Chang, one the heart disciples of the great enlightened Pabongka. Pari Dorje Chang is the past life of this present incarnation, Pari Rinpoche.[46] I think Khyongla Rato Rinpoche may also have received the oral transmission of the whole collection of Lama Tsongkhapa's teachings two times. In Tibet and afterwards, Rinpoche received oral transmissions from many great lamas, who were like the sun rising in this world, bringing unbelievable benefit to sentient beings and to the teachings of Buddha. I and the other incarnate lamas who have the time are trying to receive the lineages of many teachings, especially the rare ones, and not only from

[46] Or Dakri Rinpoche.

Khyongla Rato Rinpoche. Otherwise, after some time, the lineages might end.

How the Kopan courses started

Here at the beginning I want to say that the Kopan courses happened, basically, because of Kachen Yeshe Gyaltsen's great teaching on thought transformation, *Lojong Chenmo*, which I spent a few years reading while I was building the monastery at Lawudo. (Lama Yeshe was building Kopan Monastery at the same time.) I was supposed to be outside watching the workers to make sure they were working—I mean, there wasn't much they could do except work on building the monastery—but I spent most of my time in the cave reading Kachen Yeshe Gyaltsen's text. Sometimes, when I went outside to go to the toilet, I would check whether they were chatting or working. But even if they were chatting and not doing any work, I would just go to the toilet and go back inside.

I spent a few years reading *Lojong Chenmo*, a very extensive text on Kadampa lo-jong, or thought transformation. How did I come to get this text?

Our very first Western student was Zina Rachevsky, who had the title of "princess" in Russia. At one time I had TB, so I spent a lot of time in Darjeeling for treatment and for vacation, and I met Zina there.

I had a teacher who took care of me in Tibet, helping me to become a monk in Domo Geshe Rinpoche's monastery. Domo Geshe Rinpoche was the great lama who was Lama Govinda's guru. Lama Govinda, a German professor, went to Tibet and met Domo Geshe

Rinpoche there.[47] This is not the Domo Rinpoche who passed away
in the United States [in September 2001], but the previous incarnation. I don't know how much teaching Lama Govinda received, but
it seems that he did meet the great yogi, Domo Geshe Rinpoche.

There were a few lamas, including Domo Geshe Rinpoche, who
received complete teachings on the path to enlightenment from a
guru in Tsang, the upper part of Tibet. They lived and practiced with
their guru until one day the guru gave predictions about each disciple then sent them to a different part of Tibet. To one of them, the
guru said, "You'll go to this part of Tibet, and it will be enough for
you to be able to practice yourself." To Domo Geshe Rinpoche he
said, "You should go to the eastern part of Tibet, and you'll be able
to benefit many sentient beings."

Domo Geshe Rinpoche then went to eastern Tibet and lived
there in a forest. A shepherd from a nearby town saw a huge crea-
ture, a yeti, or abominable snowman, bringing food inside a cave to
a monk. When he told the family he worked for what he had seen,
they asked him to invite the monk to their house. It seems this was a
wealthy family in that area. The shepherd then went to the cave and
requested the lama to move down. The lama then came down from
the cave and lived in their house. The family took care of him for
about a year, and when he then asked them to build a monastery,
they built Domo Geshe's monastery near Phagri.

The main monastery had many branches in Tibet and also had
branches in Darjeeling and Sikkim. When Domo Geshe passed away,
he reincarnated in Sikkim, and it was the incarnation born in Sikkim

---

[47] See *The Way of the White Clouds.*

who passed away in the United States. There were two branches of the monastery in Darjeeling, one of which was in Ghoom, a town about five miles from Darjeeling. I went to the Ghoom monastery quite a few times and spent a long time there.

It seems that Domo Geshe Rinpoche benefited many sentient beings during his life. I didn't hear that he gave many teachings, but he made special blessed pills that were famous in Tibet. The pills were very good for people who had eaten poison by mistake, and were good for many other things. They were very powerful in blessing the body, the chakras and, of course, the mind. And if the pills were kept well, with good samaya, they also multiplied.

Domo Geshe's monastery in Tibet was where I became a monk. A senior monk from that monastery, who became the manager of the monastery, took care of me and guided me.

My story is getting longer and going deeper and deeper. I didn't mean to do that....

I don't remember the exact purpose of going to Tibet when I was young. I have many uncles: many paternal uncles, or *akus*, and many maternal uncles, or *ashangs*. One uncle lived in Tibet at Phagri, which is very close to Domo Geshe's monastery and to Bhutan. I heard that this uncle had been in the Indian army and had then gone to Tibet and married a Tibetan woman, Tsangpa. He did business in Phagri and invited us to visit him there.

At that time I was not at home with my mother but had already been away from home in Rolwaling for about seven years. Jinpa[48] is from that same place, Rolwaling. This part of Solu Khumbu is much

[48] Thubten Jinpa, a Kopan monk, is one of Rinpoche's attendants.

more primitive than the Namche Bazaar area. It's a hidden place of
Padmasambhava, but very primitive.

I was taken to Rolwaling because I used to run away home from
Thangme Monastery. I was only small, maybe four or five years old,
when I was taken up to Thangme Monastery from my home in the
village. I had to stay there to learn the alphabet from my aku, or
paternal uncle, who was a monk in Thangme Monastery. I would
stay there for a few days then escape and run down to my home.
I would just rush down the hill. Because there were some caves
and dark places at the side of the road, I would run non-stop until
I reached home. After a couple of days, someone would carry me
back up to the monastery. I did this a few times.

Since I wasn't doing a good job as a student, I was sent to Rolwaling. To reach Rolwaling, you have to cross dangerous snow
mountains where there are avalanches, crevasses and many other
obstacles. I crossed those mountains several times, though not by
myself, and nothing much happened. There was an avalanche only
one time.

I didn't have to walk; I was always carried by somebody. One
time I was carried by my teacher, Aku Ngawang Gendun, the uncle
who took care of me and taught me to read texts at Rolwaling. My
teacher carried me on his back and would pass food to me over his
shoulder.

There's one dangerous mountain that you have to cross when
you go from Rolwaling to the Namche Bazaar part of Solu Khumbu.
I remember crossing it a few times. I don't remember crossing it
going back to Rolwaling, so maybe there was another road. Before

crossing this mountain, all the people would put down their heavy loads. They would drink whatever alcohol they had and rub their hands together to generate heat. Everybody carried a huge load. Sometimes they used yaks, but because there was no proper road and there were large rocks, dealing with the yaks was unbelievably hard. They had to push the yaks in some places.

At this place, rocks, big and small, would come down from high up the mountain, and you never knew when they were coming. We would rest before crossing, and when we couldn't hear anything, everybody would lift their load and go quickly. You couldn't wait—it was a very uncertain time. At the beginning, there was a sound like "wooooohl," but I wasn't sure what it was. Later I realized that it was everybody chanting mantras and prayers. Since Sherpas are usually Nyingmapas, everybody continuously recited Padmasambhava mantras until they reached the other side. I think that's a good definition of having refuge.

If we had realization of refuge and of impermanence and death, we would never waste our time; we would never waste our life. Our mind would be in the same state as those Sherpas if we had those realizations. That day, because of the rocks coming down, the Sherpas were afraid they might die, but it is the case that death could happen any day, at any moment. If we had the realization that death could happen at any moment, our mind would be in that same state. If we had the realization of impermanence and death, we would continuously practice Dharma with our body, our speech and our mind in accordance with the level of our motivation, whether for the happiness of future lives, liberation from samsara or enlightenment.

Knowing that death could happen today, at any moment, we would prepare for it. Our mental state would be similar to that of the Sherpas, though theirs was because of the falling rocks.

If we had the realization of refuge, that Buddha, Dharma and Sangha have the power to completely protect us, we would totally rely upon them and do requesting prayers to them and prayers praising their qualities. We would also recite powerful mantras for purification. With devotion to Buddha, Dharma and Sangha, we would constantly do this with our body, speech and mind. With useful fear of samsara and especially of negative karma and the sufferings of the lower realms, we would constantly do practices to purify our defilements and negative karma and to collect extensive merit; we would do practices that become causes to achieve enlightenment, liberation from samsara and the happiness of future lives. We would never want to waste our life. Constantly, day and night, all the time, we would practice. Of course, when we slept, we would be sleeping in virtue. Because of our virtuous motivation, our sleep would be virtuous. Everything would become Dharma, pure Dharma. Even if we didn't have realization of bodhicitta or renunciation of samsara, we would still have detachment to this life and the wish to seek the happiness of future lives. That's the very minimum motivation that is Dharma.

The interesting thing here is that whenever our group had reached the other side, the rocks would then come down. The small stones would come tinnnnng–kah! And the big rocks would also come. When I had crossed I would think, "Someone must have died!" But the whole group would have completed the crossing. It was like that every time. Maybe it had something to do with the strong devotion they had to Padmasambhava, as well as to Buddha, Dharma and Sangha; but I think it might also have had to do with the protection of a protector or deva at that place.

I think I made that crossing four times, but nothing ever happened to anyone in the group. It was extremely dangerous, and I don't know why they had to go through that.

Why was I telling you about this? That's right—I was telling you the story of why I went to Tibet.

I lived in Rolwaling for seven years. In the early morning, at dawn, I would recite by heart the prayers I had memorized: various prayers to Padmasambhava, the Seventh Chapter (*lu-dunpa* in Tibetan) and other things. All day long I would recite texts. After learning to spell, I did other reading called *jo-log*. I could stop early in the evening. And we ate three or four times a day. When I went out to pee, I would hang around a little while outside.

During those times there was no sweet tea because there was no sugar. I got rice, which was regarded as a very special food, maybe two times a year. Now it has totally changed in Solu Khumbu. (I don't know how it is in the more remote parts, but they must also have changed a lot.) There have been unbelievable changes, with so many things coming in from the West. It wasn't like that when I was small, before I went to Tibet.

Rolwaling, where I lived with my paternal uncle, was a primitive place. You got rice only when a Nepalese man from a hotter place came for a few days. You might get rice to eat at the new year and during a nyung-nä. I never did a nyung-nä in Rolwaling, but my teacher would go for the nyung-näs. He would eat half of his food, then bring the other half for me to eat, so I got rice at that time. I think I ate rice twice in a year. There was no coffee or sweet tea. Nothing. In its own way, Rolwaling was completely pure before I left to go to Tibet.

I lived in Phagri for three years, and during that time Tibet was taken over by mainland China. About nine months after the takeover, we escaped to India from the Domo area. We were still doing pujas in Phagri. Every day we went to do pujas in different benefactors' houses. In one year there was maybe one day when there was no puja at all. That day seemed like a very long, very boring day. It was a strange day.

I'm not sure whether she's here in the gompa at the moment, but there's a Tibetan woman from Phagri here at Root Institute. Her name is Dekyi-la, and she has three daughters and a son. I've met her a few times in Bodhgaya. She now lives in Bhutan, where she has married into quite a wealthy family. Dekyi-la's family was one of our benefactors in Tibet. I would do puja at her family's house with my teacher at least once a month, and sometimes there were extra pujas. They could request extra pujas if they wanted.

I was young when I was there in Tibet, but what I heard was that Dekyi-la's whole family were female—even the cows and other animals were all female. One elderly woman in the family dressed up as a man and carried a small knife, Tibetan style, hanging from her belt. She owned a truck with some other people and did business in Lhasa. Her body was also a little broader, like a man's. It was only later that my teacher and the other monks told me that it wasn't a man.

There were branches of different monasteries in Phagri. One monastery was a branch of Ganden Monastery in Lhasa, another was a branch of Tashi Lhunpo Monastery and my monastery was a branch of Domo Geshe's monastery. Each monastery in the town (though in Tibet it might have been called a city) had its own benefactors, though families could be benefactors of two different monasteries.

I spent my time there in the following way. In the morning I had to memorize the texts that were recited in Domo Geshe's monastery. Then, around eight o'clock, we would pack all the things we needed—dorje, bell, damaru, text—in a bag, then go for puja. After puja, we would put everything back in our bag again, then return home. We would come back around four or five o'clock, with a stomach filled with food. So, that's what I remember.

I lived there in Domo Geshe's monastery for six months, but I think that Tibet had already been overtaken by mainland China at that time. I then escaped to India with the teacher who took care of me. After we arrived in India, because my teacher was called *changdzö-la*, which means manager, everyone thought that he was my manager. But he wasn't; he was the manager of the monastery.

The uncle who lived in Phagri invited us to come from Solu Khumbu to visit him in Tibet. That's why we went. We traveled every day on foot, apart from one day when two Tibetan men on horses had a spare horse or donkey that they let me ride for a few hours. That was the only time that I didn't have to walk. That day I arrived earlier at the house where we were to spend the night than my teachers, who had to walk with all the luggage. My two teachers, the ones who taught me to read Tibetan, were my uncles, both monks. The elder one later changed his life and took the lay aspect, but at that time he was a monk. There were one or two other people in our group.

We went to Tibet on foot, crossing the snow mountains from Solu Khumbu to Tibet, but it wasn't dangerous. It took many days, or maybe even weeks, before we arrived in Phagri. My uncle who lived in Tibet then took my two uncle-teachers to Lhasa to see Sera, Ganden and Drepung Monasteries and the Shakyamuni Buddha statue blessed by Buddha himself in the Lhasa temple. There are so many precious things in Lhasa.

I was left behind in Phagri, maybe because they thought it would be too difficult to take me to Lhasa. While they went to Lhasa, I stayed at my uncle's house in Phagri. He had married a Tibetan woman, and one of their sons was a monk in the branch monastery of Tashi Lhunpo Monastery. I was hanging around just outside the house one morning when, because of past karma, a tall monk came along and asked me, "Do you want to be my disciple?" I said, "Yes." He then went inside the house to see my aunt and told her, "He wants to be my student." They then talked together for a while. The next morning my aunt took me to his monastery, which was about fifteen minutes walk away. My aunt, who was a very good cook, had made some Tibetan tea, which she had in a thermos, and had some Tibetan bread in a Bhutanese bamboo container. She then left me there at the monastery.

My aunt had taken me there in the morning, and the monks then took me along with them to do puja that day. That first day I was asked to sit outside where the family dog was sitting. I think I was given a Yamantaka sadhana to memorize, so I sat there and memorized that. The next day I again went with them, and we did the puja together.

The idea was for me to go to Sera Monastery in Lhasa to learn debate and study. The teacher who took care of me wrote to the incarnation of Domo Geshe Rinpoche about this. The great yogi whom Lama Govinda had met had already passed away, and the incarnation, from Sikkim, was studying in central Tibet. My teacher also asked the protector of that monastery for advice, and the protector advised that I shouldn't go to Lhasa but should stay in that area.

My teacher and I then went to a small monastery called Pema Chöling between Phagri and Domo. It was a very nice place, with mountains on both sides of some flat ground and a river flowing through.

I was advised to do Lama Tsongkhapa Guru Yoga retreat by the protector of Domo Geshe's monastery. I had never received a commentary; my teacher just gave me a text, and I chanted migtsemas. I can't remember, but it seems that I did complete the required number of mantras. I offered tsog at the end of the retreat, and that night we escaped from Tibet.

Some monks from Domo Geshe's monastery had come from Phagri with a horse and cart. They brought a message about the punishment called "change by punishing," which involved beating people. It had almost arrived at Phagri and would reach our monastery after three days. So, the monks from Phagri, my teacher and I escaped that night. There were many other people working in the monastery, and some of them were spies. My teacher did a divination in front of the protector statue and said that we would be able to pass through to India though we would lose some things.

That night, my mind was very happy. I had no worry, no fear—none. In the middle of night we did some short prayers and without the rest of the people knowing (there weren't many monks in the monastery, but there were some lay people), about ten of us just quietly left. There was a little bit of snow on the ground, so when we walked, there was a crack, crack, cracking noise. Near dawn we came to some mud and some people fell over and others missed the road, but there wasn't too much trouble. Early the next morning we reached the Bhutanese area, very close to the pass. We then came to the camp of some Bhutanese nomads. We knew one of the nomad families as they used to come to Phagri, so we stayed there for seven days. From there, we went to Paro, the main city of Bhutan, where we stayed another seven days. It was there in Bhutan that I started to give out blessed strings. When we arrived at a very old temple called Kyichu Dzong, related historically to Padmasambhava, the monks from Domo Geshe's monastery went to buy some of the very cheap cloth that is used for prayer flags, and the dance of the lama started from there with my giving blessed strings to people.

My uncles took some time to make their pilgrimage to Lhasa, and while I was in Phagri, changes had already started to happen. I was doing pujas every day, and although people didn't know me as an incarnate lama, there were some rumors. My teacher then checked with the protector, and the protector responded that I was an incarnate lama and that I shouldn't eat meat or eggs.

When my uncle-teachers came back from Lhasa after some time, I was with my other teacher. My uncles then asked me whether I wanted to go back to Solu Khumbu or not. I didn't say anything, but I wrote down my answer. My elder teacher, the one from Rolwaling, then boxed my ear and made it bleed.

This uncle beat me many times when I was with him in Rolwaling. I think that all those beatings were great blessings, helping me to purify my mind. Sometimes when my teacher had gone out, I would pretend that I had read some of the text by just turning a few pages over. My teacher, coming back sooner than I expected, would know that I hadn't read all the pages I had turned. He would then beat me. He would usually hit me on the head with a piece of dry bamboo, which would shatter into pieces.

One time there had been quite a bit of rain. I don't remember what it was, but I must have done something wrong. My teacher forced my mouth down into the rainwater on the ground outside. There was a bush of nettles growing outside the door, and another time my teacher grabbed me and rubbed my back against the nettles. I don't have the impression that I found it disturbing, but it was a long time ago, so maybe I've just forgotten. I remember only a few things like that, but I think all those were great blessings, a quick way to purify my negative karma and defilements. It was a special skillful means to purify my mind.

My uncle got me to read the *Condensed Sutra,* an important

Prajnaparamita text, as well as the *Vajra-Cutter Sutra*, which I read for many months. He didn't give me any commentary on it, but just got me to recite it many times. From that, I think that much purification was done and much merit collected. I think it helped me to have now some idea of what things are empty of and of the meaning of dependent arising. I think that the tiny bit of understanding that I now have comes from those times, from the way my teacher guided me.

Of course, because I was staying with my other teacher when my uncles came back from Lhasa, things then became difficult. My uncles went to check what they should do with the secretary of a wealthy, well-known local family. The secretary, who was also a powerful benefactor of Domo Geshe's monastery, said that I should go back to Solu Khumbu. It wasn't decided by that, however, and my case then went to the district judge. All my teachers went to see the judge and discussed my case with him for some hours. The judge then asked for me to be brought there. They had taken my clothes and locked me in a very cold place, so I was shaking like a leaf in front of the judge. (I'm not sure why they took my clothes away.) The judge then gave me the right to choose whether to stay there in the monastery in Tibet or go back to Solu Khumbu.

So I continued the memorizing, pujas and other things I was supposed to do in Domo Geshe's monastery.

After we had escaped through Bhutan to India, we ended up at Buxa Duar. We weren't planning to stay at Buxa, the concentration camp where Mahatma Gandhi-ji and Nehru had been imprisoned and was a very unhealthy place. Where Mahatma Gandhi had been imprisoned became a nunnery; some nuns from Kham were put in there, I think. Where Prime Minister Nehru had been imprisoned became Sera Monastery, though not all the Sera monks could fit into that building. Both Sera Me and Sera Je monks lived inside and outside of that building. It was a very long room, with bamboo beds lined up side by side. Outside there was a verandah, and outside of that was a ditch with barbed wire. There was very little space, with the monks' beds jammed together all the way to the main door. There was one high bed outside where Geshe Rabten slept. Geshe Rabten was the first teacher to teach me Buddhist philosophy; he taught me *du-ra*, the introductory subject of Buddhist debate.

We had no plan to stay there in Buxa and intended to go to Domo Geshe's monastery in Ghoom, but the head policeman, who might have been Tibetan, stopped me from going. I'm not sure exactly why he didn't let me go to Darjeeling; it's a very interesting point. He said that I should stay there with one monk and that the other monks could go to Darjeeling. If he hadn't stopped me from going, I wouldn't have had any chance at all to hear and study a little bit of the Buddhist philosophical teachings and to see some of those texts. I wouldn't have had that chance to leave a little imprint. It was because that policeman didn't let me go to Darjeeling that I had the opportunity to live at Buxa for eight years and to do a little bit of study. We studied part of the *Abhisamayalamkara*, then a school was later established for study of the five major philosophical texts.[49]

I then got TB and went to Darjeeling for treatment, and that is

---

[49] The five major philosophical scriptures are Maitreya's *Ornament of Clear Realizations*, Dignaga's *Compendium of Valid Cognition*, Chandrakirti's *Entering the Middle Way*, Vinaya and Vasubandhu's *Treasury of Knowledge*.

where Lama Yeshe and I met Zina. She spent one month coming to the monastery where we were staying almost every morning for an hour of teachings from Lama, which I tried to translate. She then asked us to come to stay at her house so that we could more easily teach her Dharma. I think we did that for nine months. We didn't have to do much, just a little teaching in the morning.

We had only one bathroom, and Zina would spend hours there in the morning. In the early morning, she'd look like a sixty- or seventy-year-old woman. She would then spend one or two hours in the bathroom. Afterward, when she came for the teachings, she had become like a sixteen-year-old. She looked like a totally different person.

Even though she came for teachings, much of the time was spent on her telling stories of her life, of what had happened to her here and there. Some of the time was spent on her life story and some on teachings.

Zina then went to Sri Lanka and had the idea of starting a Mahayana center there. She spent a year in Sri Lanka, then came back to pick us up. We went to meet her in Calcutta; that was the first time Lama and I had been in Calcutta. We then went to Dharamsala to meet His Holiness the Dalai Lama. That was the first time we had a meeting with His Holiness in his room for instructions.

At that time Russia and India had fallen out, so there were a lot of spies following Zina. When we were traveling by train from Calcutta to Delhi, there were six Indian spies in the same compartment with us; we sat on one side and they sat on the other. They were also at our hotel in Delhi. Wherever we went, they would follow us in cars or on motorcycles or bikes. They would change vehicles according to where we were going. We met the head spy, who had a beard and a curled moustache, at the train station when we arrived in Delhi.

When Zina was ordained at Tushita, we hadn't yet bought the property. Our root guru, His Holiness Trijang Rinpoche, had lived at Tushita for seven years but then moved down to lower Dharamsala. We asked His Holiness the Dalai Lama to ordain Zina, but His Holiness was very busy and said that Lati Rinpoche should ordain her. We went to Tushita, and Lati Rinpoche ordained her there. At that time the head spy was walking back and forth, back and forth, on the road down below Tushita.

I'm not sure what happened, but we weren't able to go to Sri Lanka. It was Lama's idea that we instead go to Nepal. In Nepal, we stayed in a monastery at Boudhanath for nearly a year, then stayed in the house of Chini Lama's son. (Chini Lama was the caretaker of Boudhanath Stupa, the most precious, holy object.) There were two houses, one of which, the Double Dorje house, was near the road. Maybe it doesn't exist now—this was many years ago. There was another house near the Sakya Monastery—not His Holiness Chogye Trichen Rinpoche's monastery but the one on the other side. We stayed in that green house for almost a year.

One day a Sherpa man called Ang Nyima came to see us. He brought me Kachen Yeshe Gyaltsen's *Great Thought Transformation* text and offered Lama Yeshe the Heruka commentary composed by Pabongka's guru, Dagpo Rinpoche. Even from that time Lama never read about the generation stage; he read only about the second stage, the completion stage. I know because when Lama was out I would sometimes go into his room and check what part of the text Lama was reading.

One time we came to Bodhgaya to receive a Yamantaka commentary from His Holiness Ling Rinpoche, His Holiness the Dalai Lama's senior tutor. At that time a Zen monk had come from Scotland, and we went to the place where he was leading meditations. We all sat there for half an hour or an hour. From my analysis, I couldn't see any difference between that meditation and deep sleep.

Zina, our very first Western student, was there with us at that time, and she wanted very much for us to lead meditations like the Zen monk. She didn't want the same subject, but for us just to lead a meditation course. She requested this a few times but Lama never accepted her request. However, because I had been reading Kachen Yeshe Gyaltsen's *Great Thought Transformation* text for quite a few years, I had great interest in doing a course. When Lama wouldn't agree to do a course, Zina then asked me if I would do it. I said that I would check with Lama, who said, "If you think it will be beneficial, do it."

I did the first course in Kopan over three or four days. Basically, I was talking from *Great Thought Transformation* by Kachen Yeshe Gyaltsen, who composed this Kadampa teaching that I have here. There were one or two pages of material for people to meditate on: one or two lines on the usefulness of a perfect human rebirth and the difficulty of finding one again and six or seven lines on the sufferings of the lower realms. I think most of my talk was on perfect human rebirth.

The teaching on the last night was on bodhicitta, and somehow it seems the people liked it very much. When I later went to have dinner with Lama, Zina came up to see Lama and expressed how good the talk had been. Actually, she couldn't completely express what she felt; she couldn't believe the teaching she had heard. That's how the second and then the third courses happened.

Basically, it all came from this great lama, Kachen Yeshe Gyaltsen, who, I think, is the incarnation of Milarepa. This is according to the great yogi, His Holiness Serkong Dorje Chang, who was the incarnation of the Serkong Dorje Chang who, in Tibet, was officially recognized by the Thirteenth Dalai Lama as a great yogi who had actually reached the level where he could practice with a wisdom mother. Before that, Serkong Dorje Chang had finished all his studies and completed his geshe examination, then later he practiced with a wisdom mother. Though there were some other lamas that the Thirteenth Dalai Lama didn't accept as qualified to practice with a wisdom mother, he did officially accept Serkong Dorje Chang. There are stories about how the Thirteenth Dalai Lama punished those lamas who practiced without being qualified.

Serkong Dorje Chang, the great enlightened being who lived and passed away in Nepal, was the incarnation of that great yogi who passed away in Tibet. The incarnation of the Serkong Dorje Chang from Nepal is now studying in south India.

One time Serkong Dorje Chang was returning to his monastery at Swayambhunath after doing a puja at a benefactor's house in Kathmandu. With him there happened to be a monk from his monastery who had originally been at Sera Monastery in Tibet. It depended on the circumstances, but if it was a good day, Serkong Dorje Chang would tell stories. That day Rinpoche told this monk, "Actually, I am Marpa; Tsechokling Rinpoche[50] is Milarepa; and His Holiness Serkong Tsenshab Rinpoche is Marpa's son, Tarma Dodé."

The courses at Kopan have continued for many years—this year we had the fortieth course. After some time, it became a one-month course, and in the early times we used to do two courses a year. Then, because of traveling to the West, we could no longer do two courses, so we did only one. That has continued up to now.

The FPMT centers have basically developed from those Kopan courses. Because students found benefit to their hearts and to their lives, when they went back to the West, they wanted other people in their country to also receive the same benefit. They wanted others to not only make their lives meaningful but meet and practice Dharma and achieve enlightenment. They wanted others to see that they didn't always have to be caught up in just temporary happiness; that there are much greater things to achieve in life: the ultimate happiness of liberation and enlightenment. That's how the centers started, and there are now about 150 or 160 of them, mostly meditation centers.

Up to the sixth Kopan course, no matter what people said to me about how good a course had been, how useful for their lives, in my heart I always felt that all the benefit came from Lama Yeshe, not from me. This I what I felt from the first to the sixth courses

---

[50] The lineage of incarnations from Kachen Yeshe Gyaltsen

whenever people said how beneficial the course had been, blah, blah, blah. In my heart I felt it was Lama Yeshe, not me. I had that feeling up to the sixth or maybe seventh course. For the sixth course there were about three hundred people at the beginning, more than for other courses. I spent a lot of time on the hell realms. I talked about the lower realms and the eight worldly dharmas for two weeks, I think. Anyway, up to the sixth or seventh course, in my heart I felt that all the benefit people talked about came from Lama Yeshe. I don't know what happened after that—something must have gone wrong.

THE HEART ADVICE OF THE KADAM TEACHINGS

Kachen Yeshe Gyaltsen was the Ninth Dalai Lama's guru, and there have been many incarnations. There's a monastery built by Kachen Yeshe Gyaltsen at Kyirong in Tibet, close to the Nepalese border. It's an excellent monastery that is famous for its moral discipline. Its vinaya practice is incomparable. The main focus of this monastery is the study and practice of vinaya.

I've received the lineage of the oral transmission of *The Heart Advice of the Kadam Teachings*, though not the commentary, from Kyabje Khyongla Rato Rinpoche. The first copy of this text that I saw was given to me by Geshe Jampa Tekchog, who is the ex-abbot of Sera Je Monastery and also of our monastery in France, Nalanda, where he lived for eleven years.

The title of this text in Tibetan is *kadam leg bam gi nying po men nga dutsi bumpa tsam shi che wa shug*, or *The Heart Advice of the Kadam*

Teachings: A Fine Vase of Nectar. Bumpa tsam, a fine vase, means the wish-fulfilling vase, and *shug* means "here it is."

Generate a bodhicitta motivation by thinking, "Before what is called 'death' happens, I must ensure that I am not reborn in the lower realms and that I receive a higher rebirth. Not only that, but I must free myself from samsara. And not only that, but I must achieve enlightenment for sentient beings. Therefore, to achieve enlightenment, I am going to take this oral transmission to receive the lineage of this teaching."

The first chapter describes the qualities of the lineage lamas.

[Rinpoche gives the oral transmission of the first chapter of *The Heart Advice of the Kadam Teachings* in Tibetan. (See appendix 4 for the English translation.)]

There are eight chapters, and this first chapter contains the requesting prayer to the lineage lamas and advice on how to devote to the virtuous friend. Since there are eight chapters, I'm sorry I didn't get to start earlier.

I mentioned that the title of the text is *kadam leg bam gi nying po men nga, The Heart Advice of the Kadam Teachings. Ka* means Buddha's teachings and *dam* means the instruction that is to be practiced. So, this text is the heart advice, or instruction, of the teaching.

DEDICATIONS

> Dag gi ji nye sag päi ge wa di
> Tän dang dro wa kün la gang phän dang
> Khyä par je tsün lo zang drag pa yi
> Tän päi nying po ring du säl je shog

I dedicate whatever virtues I have ever collected

For the benefit of the teachings and of all sentient beings,

And in particular, for the essential teachings

Of perfect, pure Losang Dragpa to shine forever.

[The group recites the short mandala offering.]

Due to all the past, present and future merits collected by me and the merits of the three times collected by others, may bodhicitta be generated in my own heart, in the hearts of all the organizers, students and benefactors of the FPMT, especially those many people in different parts of the world who sacrifice themselves to the organization and bear so much hardship in offering service to sentient beings and the teaching of the Buddha, in the hearts of all the people who rely upon me, for whom I have promised to pray and whose names have been given to me and in the hearts of all the rest of the sentient beings.

As I mentioned the other day, when you look at the ocean from a plane, you know that inside the ocean there are all those whales, sharks and other large animals, as well as many tiny ones. The ocean is full of animals, including all those tiny animals that you can see only through a microscope. It's unbelievable. And there is so much suffering, with all those animals looking for food and killing each other.

It is similar with the animals in the air and on and under the ground. Just among animals there is unbelievable suffering. Also, there are the hungry ghosts, who are as numerous as trees in a forest or blades of grass in a field. And the hell beings are like the dust of this earth. Human beings are experiencing the oceans of suffering of the human realm, and the asuras and suras are experiencing the oceans of suffering of their realms.

Dedicate that all these beings generate bodhicitta in their hearts without even a second's delay, and that those in whose hearts bodhicitta has already been generated increase it. Please pray in this way.

> Jang chhub sem chhog rin po chhe
> Ma kye pa nam kye gyur chig
> Kye wa nyam pa me pa yang
> Gong nä gong du phel war shog

> May the supreme jewel bodhicitta
> That has not arisen, arise and grow;
> And may that which has arisen not diminish
> But increase more and more.

> Due to all the merits of the three times collected by me
> and by others, may bodhicitta be generated in the hearts
> of all the world leaders.

In that way the many millions of people in each country won't suffer and will be led in the correct path to peace and happiness.

> May the loving, compassionate thought of bodhicitta be
> actualized in the hearts of all the believers, the people of

different religions, and of all the non-believers without even a second's delay.

[Everyone recites *Jang chhub sem chhog rin po chhe*.... two more times.]

Gang ri ra wäi khor wäi zhing kham dir

Phän dang de wa ma lü jung wäi nä

Chän rä zig wang tän dzin gya tsho yi

Zhab pä si thäi bar du tän gyur chig

In the land encircled by snow mountains

You are the source of all happiness and good;

All-powerful Chenrezig, Tenzin Gyatso,

Please remain until samsara ends.

We will now dedicate all the merits collected in the three times by ourselves and by others, which means all sentient beings and all buddhas, for all the holy wishes that His Holiness has to be completely actualized without even a second's delay.

Tong nyi nying je zung du jug päi lam

Chhe chher säl dzä gang chän tän droi gon

Chhag na pä mo tän dzin gya tsho la

Sol wa deb so zhe don lhun drub shog

Savior of the Snow Land teachings and transmigratory
   beings,

Who makes extremely clear the path that is the unification
   of emptiness and compassion,
To the Lotus Holder, Tenzin Gyatso, I beseech—
May all your holy wishes be spontaneously fulfilled.

Make the same prayer for the other gurus. May all their wishes be
fulfilled and may they have stable life.

Je tsün la mäi ku tshe rab tän ching
Nam kar thrin lä chhog chur gyä pa dang
Lo zang tän päi drön me sa sum gyi
Dro wäi mün sel tag tu nä gyur chig

May my perfect, pure lama's life be firm,
His white divine actions spread in the ten directions.
May the torch of the teachings of Losang always remain,
Dispelling the darkness of all beings in the three realms.

[The students recite Rinpoche's short long-life prayer.]

Due to all the past, present and future merits collected by
me and the merits of the three times collected by others,
may all the father and mother sentient beings have happiness, especially the ultimate happiness of enlightenment; may the three lower realms be empty of beings
forever; may all the bodhisattvas' prayers succeed immediately; and may I be able to cause all this to happen by
myself alone.

Due to all the past, present and future merits collected by me and the merits of the three times collected by others, in all lifetimes may I, all my family members, all the students and benefactors of the FPMT organization, especially those who bear so much hardship in dedicating their lives to this organization to serve sentient beings and the teaching of Buddha, and all the rest of the sentient beings meet only perfectly qualified Mahayana gurus. From my side and from the side of each sentient being, in all lifetimes may we be able to see the guru as only an enlightened being, having ceased all faults and perfected all qualities; may we be able to do actions that are only most pleasing to the holy mind of the virtuous friend; and may we be able to accomplish the holy wishes of the virtuous friend.

Due to all the past, present and future merits collected by me and the merits of the three times collected by others, may all the projects to serve monasteries and nunneries and those who preserve and spread Dharma by providing food, money, education needs and so forth continue and flourish forever.

Due to all the merits of the three times collected by me and by others, may all the projects to build holy objects such as statues and stupas, and especially all the Maitreya Buddha statues in different parts of the world, be completed as quickly as possible and be most beneficial to all sentient beings. (This is the quickest way to purify the negative karma and defilements of sentient beings, enable them to collect extensive merit and bring them to enlightenment.)

May all the various social service projects in different parts of the world—Liberation Prison Project, Essential Education, the hospices, clinics dispensing medicine, Loving Kindness Peaceful Youth—be accomplished immediately by receiving all the necessary funding and other needs. May all these projects be accomplished and be most beneficial for all sentient beings, causing compassion to be generated in the hearts of the people who receive their services. (By generating compassion, they will collect merit; they will then change their mind and their actions, creating good karma, and then achieve enlightenment as quickly as possible.) May they achieve enlightenment as quickly as possible. May all the various social service projects in different parts of the world receive everything they need to be most beneficial to sentient beings.

May all the meditation centers be most beneficial for all sentient beings, and may whatever social service and other projects each center has be accomplished and be most beneficial for sentient beings. May they cause sentient beings to generate faith in Buddha, Dharma and Sangha and in karma, action and result, and, especially, to generate loving kindness, compassion and bodhicitta in their hearts. Especially, may the centers spread the complete teaching of Lama Tsongkhapa in the hearts of all sentient beings. May they be most beneficial in this way.

Due to all the past, present and future merits collected by me and the merits of the three times collected by others, which exist but which are totally empty from their own side, may the I, who exists but who is totally empty from its own side, achieve Guru Shakyamuni Buddha's enlightenment, which exists but which is totally empty from its own side, and lead all the sentient beings, who exist but who are totally empty from their own side, to that Guru Shakyamuni Buddha's enlightenment, which exists but which is totally empty from its own side, by myself alone, who exists but who is totally empty from its own side.

I dedicate all these merits in the best way, that I may be able to follow the holy extensive deeds of the bodhisattvas Samantabhadra and Manjugosha, who realized things as they are.

I dedicate all these merits in the same way the buddhas of the three times dedicate their merits.

Tonight we will recite the lam-rim dedication. Dedicate in the way that you see there in the English translation. Dedicate the merits for

the lam-rim to be generated within your own heart, in the hearts
of your family and in the hearts of everybody in this world, so that
everyone has perfect peace and happiness.

[All chant *Final Lam-Rim Prayer* in Tibetan.]

> Chhö kyi gyäl po tsong kha päi
> Chhö tshül nam par phäl wa la
> Geg kyi tshän ma zhi wa dang
> Thün kyen lü tshang war shog

> By pacifying all the signs of obstacles
> And by perfecting every single required condition
> May the Dharma tradition of the Dharma king Tsongkhapa
> Be preserved and developed.

> Dag dang zhän gyi dü sum dang
> Drel wä tshog nyi la ten nä
> Gyäl wa lo zang drag pa yi
> Tän pa yün ring bar gyur chig

> Due to the two types of merit collected
> Over the three times by myself and others,
> May the teaching of the far-famed
> Victorious One's pure wisdom blaze forth.

So, good night or good morning. No, good night!

December 29

I must apologize that at this time I didn't get to do much teaching, though I did begin the oral transmission of the Kadam text, *The Heart Advice of the Kadam Teachings*. I think I will first translate it into English, and then teach on at another time. Since I have received the lineage, I thought to give the oral transmission of the text, which will plant the seed of the whole path to enlightenment.

I gave the oral transmission of the first chapter, which contains the qualities of the lineage lamas and guru devotion. As the subjects covered in this text are quite extensive, I will just pass the oral transmission. Or maybe I will read just the section on guru devotion, as it's not too long, so that there's some teaching. I'll leave out the part on the qualities of the lineage lamas.

We'll start with a short motivation. As I mentioned before, the whole point of our life is to benefit others. Therefore, we must free the numberless sentient beings from the oceans of samsaric suffering and bring them happiness, especially the ultimate happiness of liberation from samsara and especially full enlightenment. Think, "To be able to do that, I must achieve the state of omniscient mind. For that, I need to actualize the steps of the path to enlightenment, and so, as a preparation for those realizations, I'm going to take the oral transmission of the great enlightened being Kachen Yeshe Gyaltsen's *The Heart Advice of the Kadam Teachings: A Fine Vase of Nectar*."

GURU DEVOTION

> Please grant me blessings to be able to correctly devote to
> the virtuous friend, who reveals the excellent, unmistaken
> path and upon whose power depends every single collec-
> tion of goodness of samsara and peace.

Here *peace* isn't what is normally regarded as peace in newspapers and on TV. Here it refers to ultimate happiness, to liberation
from samsara and enlightenment. In the Tibetan expression *si-zhi*,
si means samsaric existence and *zhi* means the peace that is the
opposite of samsara, the ultimate happiness of liberation and also
enlightenment.

Every single collection of goodness of samsara and peace definitely depends on whose power? The power of the virtuous friend.
It is for this reason that we need to correctly devote ourselves to the
virtuous friend, who reveals the excellent, unmistaken path. Therefore, we request to be granted blessings to be able to do that.

Many of you have heard teachings on guru devotion many times,
but I think some people are hearing Buddhadharma for the first time,
so this subject will be new to them. Some people might have some
difficulties understanding guru devotion, but you should know that
there are many new things awaiting discovery. On TV there's the
Discovery Channel, which has programs about discoveries in Africa
and many other parts of the world. There are so many things in this
world (I'm not talking about in other worlds) that we are not aware
of, that we have yet to discover. Now this Discovery Channel here

is showing the path to be actualized in your heart, the path that removes all the sufferings, all the different levels of defilements, all the faults of the mind, and enables you to achieve full enlight enment. There are many stages that you have to discover, that you have to learn about. You must expect to make many discoveries on this Discovery Channel, the enlightenment channel. Since the path to enlightenment is a whole new path, you must expect to have a lot to learn, and you must open your heart to that. You shouldn't have a closed mind, thinking that just knowing one or two meditations in your life will be enough. You shouldn't think like that because you have so much wisdom, so much intelligence. If you think like that, you're wasting your intelligence; you're not using your capacity.

> Since you normally check whether you can trust some-
> one who will guide you through a dangerous place even
> for a single day, how can you be satisfied to trust just
> anybody to show you the path that goes to the heart of
> enlightenment?

The first part of this verse isn't talking about the virtuous friend. It's saying that even when we travel for a day along a dangerous road, we check the person who guides us.

> The qualities of a guru who reveals the path are men-
> tioned by the Victorious Ones in many sutras and tantras.
> Having examined him well with an impartial mind, rely
> on a virtuous friend who has the ten qualities.

An impartial mind means one that isn't biased by discriminating thoughts of anger or attachment. It's a straight mind that doesn't take sides. With that mind you examine the guru well.

The ten qualities are normally used as examples of a guru's qualities:

> Rely upon a virtuous friend who is subdued, pacified and
>   highly pacified,
> Has greater knowledge, has perseverance, is learned in
>   scripture,
> Has realized emptiness, is skillful in teaching,
> Has a compassionate nature and has abandoned
>   discouragement.[51]

Has greater knowledge can mean having greater education but it can also mean having greater qualities.

Of course, I myself don't have these ten qualities—it would be hard to find even one of these qualities in me. I think it's just that it's such a degenerate time and there's some karma....

Here it's saying to rely on a virtuous friend who has the ten qualities. That's the normal instruction, but these days, as we don't see gurus with all ten qualities, it's advised to rely on a guru with seven, six, five or even fewer of the qualities.

The first quality, *subdued*, refers to the higher training of morality. The second, *pacified*, refers to the higher training of concentration. The third, *highly pacified*, refers to the higher training of wisdom. The

[51] From *Ornament of Mahayana Sutras* by Maitreya Buddha. For further details see *The Heart of the Path* by Lama Zopa Rinpoche, pp. 32-33.

following qualities are having higher qualities, having perseverance, having a holy mind that is enriched with understanding of the
teachings, having realized emptiness....

The reason that having realized emptiness is mentioned even
though the higher training of wisdom has already been mentioned
is that here it refers specifically to the Madhyamaka, or Middle Way,
view. There are four schools of Buddhist philosophy: Vaibhashika,
Sautrantika, Chittamatra and Madhyamaka, and the Madhyamaka
school has two subdivisions, Svatantrika and Prasangika.

To be completely liberated from the entire ocean of samsaric suffering and its cause, actions (or karma) and disturbing thoughts,
you have to cut the root of samsara: the ignorance that holds the
I and the aggregates on which the I is labeled to be truly existent.
(The Tibetan term *nyon mong* is often translated as "disturbing
thoughts," but I prefer to translate it as "obscuring, disturbing negative attitudes.") So, the root of all those obscuring, disturbing negative attitudes is the ignorance that holds the I and the aggregates
to be truly existent, that holds them to exist as they appear to exist,
which means as real in the sense of existing from their own side,
or existing by their nature. We need to cut, to eliminate, this ignorance. However, it can be eliminated *only* by the view of the second
Madhyamaka school, the Prasangika. The Prasangika understanding of emptiness, which unifies emptiness and dependent arising, is
the only one that can eliminate this ignorance.

For example, while I, action, object and all other phenomena
exist, they are empty, empty of existing from their own side. To
explain how things exist, His Holiness the Dalai Lama often uses

the term *ten jung*, and this term is also often mentioned in the philosophical texts. Basically, these two words, *ten* and *jung*, describe how things exist. By understanding *ten* and *jung*, you see the Middle Way devoid of the two extremes;[52] you see how things exist.

My talk is becoming a little long, and this is extra explanation, but anyway....

EXAMPLES OF DEPENDENT ARISING

Kyabje Khunu Lama Rinpoche was the great bodhisattva from whom His Holiness received the elaborate commentary to *A Guide to the Bodhisattva's Way of Life*. Many years ago Rinpoche was teaching *A Guide to the Bodhisattva's Way of Life* in the Tibetan Monastery in Bodhgaya, not in the main gompa but in a room upstairs where he and many other incarnate lamas used to stay when taking teachings from His Holiness the Dalai Lama or from Ling Rinpoche. Many of us stayed upstairs in that room. Lama Yeshe was there and also Geshe Jampa Gyatso, resident teacher at Istituto Lama Tzong Khapa in Italy for more than twenty years. There were many other incarnate lamas and other geshes, including Geshe Jampa Gyatso's teacher, Geshe Tashi Bum. Geshe Jampa Gyatso was cooking for and serving Geshe Tashi Bum. This was many years ago.

Anyway, when Kyabje Khunu Rinpoche was giving a commentary to *A Guide to the Bodhisattva's Way of Life*, attended by many incarnate lamas and geshes, Rinpoche used his fingers to illustrate

---

[52] Eternalism and nihilism.

dependent arising. When you hold up just your middle and ring fingers, the middle finger is long and the ring finger is short. But when you change and hold up just your ring and little fingers, the ring finger becomes long. This is how Rinpoche introduced the concept of dependent arising, *ten jung*.

If the ring finger were a real long finger, in the sense of one existing from its own side, it should always be a long finger. When you hold it up with the middle finger, it should still be a long finger. Do you understand the point? If the long ring finger weren't merely imputed by the mind, if it existed from its own side, it should still be a long finger when you hold it next to the middle finger. But it's not. When you hold up your middle finger with your ring finger, it's totally different. The middle finger is then long and the ring finger is short. So, this shows that nothing exists from its own side, that long and short are merely imputed by the mind.

Here the meaning of "merely imputed by the mind" is clear; it means there's nothing existing from its own side. That's what we have to discover, to realize.

Take the example of a family, with a father and mother and a child. Let's say the child is a daughter. That child is the daughter of her mother and father, but when she herself has a child of her own, she will be the mother to that child. Again, if a real daughter existed from its own side, she couldn't become a mother; she couldn't change. But, since "daughter" is merely imputed by the mind, when she has children, she can become "mother." So, it's dependent. The label is merely imputed by mind in dependence upon conditions. There's nothing real there, nothing that exists from its own side.

That child is a daughter in relation to her mother and father, but when she gets married and has children of her own, she becomes a mother in relation to her children. So, what exists is what is merely imputed by the mind.

It's the same, of course, with fat and skinny, though maybe it's better if I don't use actual people as the examples. However, I'm fat compared to somebody thinner than I am; but if somebody is fatter than I am, I'm then thin. Again, the label is imputed by the mind in dependence upon conditions. There's nothing there existing from its own side, nothing at all. Not even an atom exists from its own side.

It is the same with beautiful and ugly. Whether it's a drawing or a person, if it's ugly, when there's another drawing or person that is much uglier, that drawing or person becomes beautiful. The person becomes beautiful in dependence upon somebody else who is more ugly. And if somebody else is more beautiful, this person becomes ugly. So, what exists is what is merely imputed by the mind. There's nothing there that exists from its own side; it's simply labeled.

It is like this with all phenomena. Nothing exists from its own side, nothing exists apart from what is merely imputed by the mind. You can find many similar examples.

HOW TIME EXISTS

The next example that I'm going to mention is a very good meditation on emptiness. It's simple but profound, and gives us a clear understanding.

When we hear or think of one year, "Oh, it takes one year to do that," whether it's study or travel, it's a real one year, one that exists from its own side. Now, when you analyze that one year, you find that it is labeled on the base, twelve months. "One year" is imputed by your mind to the base, twelve months.

So, what is one year? Twelve months. Twelve months is what is called "one year." When we think of the base, the twelve months, it's not that one year becomes totally nonexistent. One year exists, but it exists in mere name, merely imputed by the mind. It's not that it becomes totally nonexistent. It's not that there's no one year. There is one year, but it is something unbelievably subtle. What one year is is extremely subtle. It's not that it doesn't exist at all. It exists, but what it is is unbelievably subtle, unbelievably fine. Thinking of the base, the twelve months, gives some idea of how very subtle the one year is.

The one year that you thought of at the beginning doesn't exist. The real one year that you thought of without thinking of the twelve months, the real one year existing from its own side, is not there. It doesn't exist. That one doesn't exist at all, anywhere. It's not on the tip of your nose, nor anywhere else. I'm joking. It exists nowhere.

When you think of the base, the twelve months, your understanding of one year is something totally different from what appeared to you and what you believed before. It's not that real one at all. The one year still exists. It's not nonexistent; it exists, but it's empty, empty of existing from its own side. It's empty of the year that you first thought of, that first appeared to you and in which you believed. When you think of the twelve months, the one year exists but it's now something totally different from what you thought before, from what appeared to you and what you believed before. It's totally different. It exists but it's empty. It exists but it's unified with emptiness. So, this is the Middle Way.

It is the same with the month. When we think of a month, what comes to our mind is a real month in the sense of one existing from its own side. If we had to describe the meaning of real, we would say "existing from its own side." Now what is that month? It is imputed to four weeks. Again here it comes to the same point: a month is imputed to, or labeled on, the base, the four weeks. It is never the month that appeared to us and that we believed in before, the real month existing from its own side. It is never that at all—it is totally something else, something that is labeled on the base, the four weeks.

Again here, the month is that which is merely imputed by the mind to the valid base, four weeks. It is not that one month becomes nonexistent, but for your mind it becomes extremely subtle, unbelievably subtle. It exists in mere name, merely imputed by mind. Again, it exists but it unifies emptiness and dependent arising, which is the Middle Way view. The one month you believed in previously, something that appeared to you as existing from its own side and that you believed existed from its own side, is the eternal one. Now, when you think of the four weeks, of how the one month is merely imputed to the valid base, four weeks, the one month is empty of eternalism and nihilism. It's empty of eternalism, the real one month existing from its own side, and also empty of nihilism, the nonexistence of the one month. This is the Middle Way. The one month exists but at the same time it's empty; these two are unified.

The previous one month that appeared to you as something real and in which you believed is false; that is what doesn't exist. The second one month, the imputed one month, exists. It is not nonexistent; it exists, but it exists in mere name, merely imputed by the mind. So, it unifies emptiness and dependent arising. That is what exists.

Now, the week. When you think of a week, "Oh, this course takes one week," you think of a real week existing from its own side. A real week appears to you and your mind also believes in it. Now, the week is merely imputed to the valid base, seven days. Again, what you discover here is that the week is totally different from the one that appeared to you and in which you believed before when you didn't analyze it. That week is a false week, that week is totally nonexistent. When you don't analyze, when you don't check, it looks as if the week is existing from its own side; but when you analyze, you find it's the total opposite. When you analyze, there's no such week there. The week that exists is what is merely imputed by the mind to the seven days. That's the week that exists. The week exists in mere name, merely imputed by mind, because there are the seven days. So, the week exists but it's extremely subtle. While it's empty it's existing.

Now, the day. When you think of a day, how does the day appear to you? How the day appears to you and how you believe it to exist is as a real day in the sense of one existing from its own side. It doesn't appear to you as existing from the side of your mind, but from its own side. There is a real day. But the next question is, What exactly is that one day? It is what is simply imputed by the mind because there are the twenty-four hours.

Now, here, when you think of the valid base, the twenty-four hours, to which the day is merely imputed by your mind, you see that one day is totally empty of the day that first appeared to you and that your mind believed in. It's completely empty of that. The day that appeared to you and in which you believed at the very beginning is false. Ignorance believes that it exists, but in reality it doesn't exist at all; there's no such thing. The second day, the imputed day, is extremely subtle, unbelievably subtle. It's not completely nonexistent; it exists, but it's empty of existing from its own side, as you first believed. So, that's the day that exists.

Now, the hour. When you think of an hour, again you think of something existing from its own side and believe it to be true. So, what is an hour? It's what is merely imputed by the mind because there's the valid base, sixty minutes. When you think of that, your understanding of an hour is something totally other than what appeared to you and you believed in before, that inherently existent hour, that hour existing from its own side, that real hour from its own side. It has totally changed. The previous one becomes totally nonexistent when you come to analyze what an hour is and find it is what is merely imputed by your mind because there is the valid base, sixty minutes. So, the hour becomes extremely subtle. It's not that it doesn't exist, but it becomes like that, like it doesn't exist. Saying "like that" makes a big difference. It is something extremely subtle. It's not that it doesn't exist; it's not that it's nonexistent. It exists but it's something extremely subtle. It exists in mere name, merely imputed by mind. It's empty of existing from its own side.

o now, the minute. A minute has sixty seconds, but when we think of a minute we think of a real minute existing from its own side. So, that's the *gak-cha*, the object to be refuted. When we analyze what that minute is, we find that it is what exists in mere name, merely imputed by the mind, because there is the valid base, sixty seconds. It's extremely subtle. It's not that it doesn't exist, but it's like it doesn't exist. There's a huge difference between this one and the previous false one, which is the object to be refuted. This is the reality. It's not that it doesn't exist, but it's like it doesn't exist. The way it exists is unbelievably subtle.

Now, the second. The parts of a second are extremely fine. In his teachings, the great, enlightened Pabongka explained that according to the first school, the Vaibhashika, a Lesser Vehicle school, the duration of a finger-snap is sixty-five moments. But according to the Mahayana, there are 365 moments in a finger-snap. The four schools of Buddhist philosophy have different explanations, with some believing that atoms don't have parts, for example. However, the Prasangika-Madhyamaka school believes that the continuity of consciousness has parts, that there are 365 moments in a finger-snap and that atoms have particles. The different schools have different ways of explaining things.

Anyway, a finger-snap exists in mere name, merely imputed by the mind, because there are all these sixty-five or 365 moments. (You need to check whether or not the divisions of a second can become much finer still.)

However, the main point here is that when you analyze in this way, you come to know what is false and what is the reality in relation to one year, one month, one week, one day, one hour, one minute, one second. In this way what exists and what doesn't exist become very clear.

So, I think we will just leave it there....

Green Tara who spoke to Atisha, on the Mahabodhi Stupa

Wendy Cook

Appendixes

. . .

Ven. Ailsa Cameron (editor of this book) and Ven. Trisha Labdron (director of Root Institute) at the Mahabodhi Stupa, Bodhgaya

Wendy Cook

Mind Training Removing Obstacles

Homage to the greatly compassionate spiritual teachers!

[The instruction on] dispelling the obstacles of Mahayana mind training is, it has been taught, (1) to accept ill omens as charms, (2) to exterminate Mara at its very source, (3) to bring obstacles onto the path, and (4) to cap your least useful desires.

1. *First, [accepting all ill omens as charms] is as follows:* When worldly people encounter bad omens, such as hearing owls crying or foxes howling [at night], they consult astrology, make divinations, and have rituals performed. You, on the other hand, should eagerly embrace ill omens and negative signs when they appear by cultivating the thought "Since it is self-grasping that causes me to suffer, may all the suffering that exists in the world arising from the fear of encountering ill omens befall upon this self. May this help vanquish the self-grasping."

2. *Second, [exterminating Mara at its very source] is as follows:* It is taught that self-grasping causes us to suffer. So when you experience pain or injury to your bodies, caused either by humans or nonhumans, you should think, "It is this [body] that causes me to undergo suffering.

If you desire it, take it away this very instant. O king of demons residing above, take away my head! Great indeed is your kindness in causing all the harms to it. Since you are my ally in subduing the [true] enemy, and my ally in subduing Mara, help me exterminate the very continuum of worldly gods, humans, and ghosts, and help me to vanquish [this] demon to the best of my ability." Cut [self-grasping] from its root with the thought "It is not inconsistent to relish doing so."

3. *Third, [bringing obstacles onto the path] is as follows:* Whatever unhelpful events, such as physical ailments, mental anxieties, and so on, occur, or when adversities afflict you, contemplate, "This is due to my own self-grasping. If today I do not discard this self-grasping, obstacles will continue to arise. So may all the adversities in the world and those feared to come be realized upon me. May this help subdue the self and utterly destroy it." Contemplating thus, bring them onto the path.

4. *Fourth, [capping one's desires that are least useful] is as follows:* "What benefit has this brought me, if any? It has never made me go farther away from cyclic existence, so it must be destroyed [today]. Then, at least, I will have derived some purpose from its utter lack of usefulness. [If I achieve this,] it will be due to my teacher's blessing; it will be owing to his kindness. Pray help me so that in the future, too, I can gather upon this [self-grasping] everything that has no usefulness and vanquish them by subjugating them." Contemplating in this way, cap your least useful desires.

Colophon

From *Mind Training: The Great Collection*, pp. 239–40.

The Jewel Rosary of the Practice of Bodhicitta

I bow down to great compassion,
To all my spiritual masters,
And to my deities of devotion.

Having cast away all my doubts
About the value of spiritual practice,
I shall exert myself in the practice
Of the bodhisattva path.

Having removed sleepiness, dullness and laziness,
I shall always be joyful
When engaging in such incredible practices.

I shall guard the doors of my speech, body and mind
Against any negative action,
By constantly being alert and mindful in my behavior.
I shall examine my mind
Over and over again, day and night.

I proclaim my faults, not seeking faults in others,

Hide my own good qualities but praise those of others.

Not seeking material gain or veneration from others,

I will be able to abandon any desire for fame,

Being content with whatever I have.

I shall not fail to repay whatever kindness

I receive from others

And shall meditate on love and compassion,

Reminding myself always of bodhicitta,

The altruistic mind of enlightenment.

I abandon the ten nonvirtuous actions

And consolidate my faith in spiritual practice.

Having abandoned pride over my qualities

And disdain towards others,

Always humble,

I abandon wrong livelihood and follow right livelihood.

Having given up all meaningless activity,

I shall be endowed

With the inner jewel of arya beings.

Having given up all meaningless activity,

I remain in solitude,

Abandon senseless talk

And discipline my speech.

Whenever I see my spiritual master

I pay respect from my heart,

And with equal respect
Hold even ordinary sentient beings to be my great teachers,
As I hold great arya beings to be.

Whenever I meet others
I regard older ones as my parents,
Those of similar age or younger
As my brother, sister or relative.

Having abandoned bad influence from others,
I shall follow spiritual friends,
Be happy myself wherever I go,
Without any ill will towards others,
And not be discontented with my life.

I abandon attachment to any desirable things
And remain desireless,
For attachment in any form
Can never lead to a happy rebirth.
Instead, it takes away the life-force
Of liberation from suffering.

I shall exert myself in any virtuous activity
That can lead me to ultimate happiness,
Accomplishing first whatever practices I have started.
Thus, I will be able to accomplish all my practices,
Otherwise none of my tasks will be accomplished.
I take no interest in those activities

That can be harmful to others,

And cast away pride over my qualities

Whenever it arises in my mind.

I must remind myself always

Of the instructions of my spiritual teacher.

I shall be able to encourage myself

Whenever I feel depressed,

Whenever my mind is deluded by attachment to myself

And hatred towards others,

I shall be able to realize that both I and others

Are equally void of inherent existence,

And view myself and others

As being illusory-like, a magic form.

Whenever I hear unpleasant words,

I view them as echoes.

Whenever my body is harmed by others,

I shall be able to view it as being

The result of my previous negative karma.

Abiding always in solitude,

Like the corpse of a wild animal,

I shall keep myself away from the temptation

Of meaningless activities,

And remain desireless,

Reminding myself always of my deity of devotion.

Whenever laziness or laxity arise in my mind,

I shall be able to remove them immediately

And always remember the essence of moral behavior.

Whenever I meet others,

Having removed angry behavior,

I shall be able to speak sincerely and frankly,

With a smiling face.

Whenever I meet others,

I shall not be jealous of them,

But be generous to them.

I abandon any dispute with others

And concern myself with their welfare and comfort.

I shall not be fickle in any relationships with others,

But remain firm.

I give up any form of humiliating others

And always respect them.

Whenever I give advice to others,

I shall do so with sincerity and sympathy.

I abandon any disrespect for other forms of spiritual practice

And appreciate whatever religions others are interested in.

I shall be able to remain with the practice of the ten virtues, day
   and night.

I shall dedicate whatever virtues I have done in the past,

Do now and will do in the future,
To the benefit of other sentient beings.

Through performing the seven-limb prayer
I pray for the happiness of all other beings.

Thus I will be able to accomplish
The merit of wisdom and skillful means,
And will be able to eliminate all delusions,
For in this way,
I shall be able to attain enlightenment
For the sake of all sentient beings.
Thus I will be able to achieve great meaning
From finding this precious human rebirth.

There are seven gems that adorn the minds of bodhisattvas:
The gem of faith,
The gem of instruction,
The gem of contemplation,
The gem of wisdom,
The gem of ethics,
The gem of modesty,
And the gem of generosity.

These seven gems have limitless virtuous qualities.
When I practice these inner gems within myself,
I should not reveal any to those
Who are not yet mature to practice these excellent qualities.

I shall be heedful of my speech

In the presence of others,

And be heedful of my thoughts

In isolation from others.

Colophon

Composed by Lama Atisha, translated by Geshe Namgyal Wangchen. See *Step by Step*, pp. 126–130.

Buddha statue in the main shrine room of the Mahabodhi Stupa

Wendy Cook

The Real Meaning of Guru

I F YOU UNDERSTAND the actual meaning of the guru, you don't see any difference between the deity and the guru; you can't separate the deity and the guru. If you understand what the guru really means, you discover that they're one. Therefore, when we hear the word "guru" or think of the guru, we shouldn't think that it is something separate from the deity—and this is not only during guru devotion meditation when we are doing analysis, by using logical reasoning and by remembering quotations, to try to prove to our mind, which sees the guru and buddha as two separate things, that they are one. The main meditation is trying to discover that the guru and buddha are one. Even though there are two different names, they're one thing.

You train your mind by doing analytic meditation on how the guru is buddha; when you come to the conclusion that the guru is buddha, you then keep your mind one-pointedly in that discovery or experience, understanding that these two are one. You then keep your mind on that conclusion for as long as you can. This is fixed meditation. By training your mind in this way, by doing analytical and fixed meditation together, your realization that guru and buddha are one gradually becomes stable. It doesn't change. For your mind it's unshakable, indestructible. Your devotion seeing the guru as buddha becomes very stable.

When day and night, all the time, this is what your heart spontaneously, effortlessly, experiences, this is the realization of guru devotion. This is what causes you to receive all the blessings of the guru or of the deity, which is the same thing. From that you are then able to achieve all the realizations from the graduated path of the being of lower capability, which starts with perfect human rebirth, to the graduated path of the being of middling capability, to the graduated path of the being of higher capability, which includes the tantric path, up to enlightenment.

When you see the guru, when you think of the guru, when you recite a prayer with the word "guru," the understanding should come in your heart that this is the dharmakaya, the buddha's holy mind, the primordial mind which has no beginning and no end, which pervades all phenomena, and which is bound with infinite compassion for sentient beings. Whenever the karma of a sentient being to receive guidance has ripened, no matter where that sentient being is, without even a second's delay, this can manifest in any form that accords with that sentient being's karma and give guidance. Without any superstitious thought, this works spontaneously, effortlessly, for sentient beings, even though they are numberless. It is like the sun. There's only one sun in the world, but when it rises it is reflected in every body of water—oceans, rivers, and even drops of dew—as long as it isn't covered. The sun doesn't have the motivation, "I'm going to be reflected in all the drops of dew in this beautiful garden or in this country." The sun doesn't have such a plan.

This is the example usually given in the teachings: there is only one sun but when it rises it is reflected in every body of water that is uncovered. Like that, the guru is able to benefit all the numberless sentient beings. Therefore, the guru manifests as Shakyamuni Buddha, founder of the present Buddhadharma in this world. The guru also manifests as all the lineage lamas, as well as the deities of the four classes of tantra, and reveals the path to achieve enlightenment of each deity. The guru manifests as the thousand buddhas of this eon; as the Medicine Buddhas, who are very powerful for success if sentient beings pray to them, make offerings to them, or recite their names or mantras; as the Thirty-five Buddhas, who are very powerful in purifying negative karma. The guru manifests in all these aspects of buddha, who have different functions. Even among the Thirty-five Buddhas, each buddha purifies specific negative karmas.

Relate all this to yourself. The guru has manifested to you in all of them, including Guru Shakyamuni Buddha, who taught 84,000 teachings—pratimoksha, Mahayana sutra (Paramitayana) and Mahayana tantra—and revealed the whole path to enlightenment. It manifested also in the forms of bodhisattvas, such as Chenrezig, Manjushri, Kshitigarbha, and the rest of the eight bodhisattvas. It manifested in the forms of arhats, such as the Sixteen Arhats. It manifested in the forms of dakas and dakinis, and it manifested in the forms of protectors. To guide you, the guru manifested all the many beings in the merit field. They are all manifested for you. The guru manifested in all these many aspects to perform different actions to guide you, to help you to actualize the path and cross the ocean of samsara, to bring you to enlightenment.

The guru doesn't manifest in only the merit field that you visualize for meditation. The guru manifests in any form that's needed by you and by any other sentient being. The guru manifests in all sorts of forms, even animal forms. The guru manifests in the forms of beggars, who cause you to collect merit. The guru manifests in all kinds of forms to guide you, to help you.

So, this is the absolute guru. This is what we have to remember here. The real meaning of guru is the absolute guru, the dharmakaya, the holy mind of all the buddhas.

There is the absolute guru and the conventional guru. We need the ordinary aspect of the conventional guru to guide us because we don't have the karma to be able to see the guru in the pure aspect of a buddha, without any faults, sufferings, delusions, or mistakes in their actions. Since we don't yet have the karma to see the guru in the aspect of buddha, we need an ordinary aspect to guide us. *Ordinary aspect* means having faults, having the sufferings of old age, sickness, and so forth, having delusions, and making mistakes in their actions. This is what *ordinary aspect* means. Since we have only the karma to see and receive guidance from an ordinary aspect, the only way that the absolute guru, which is bound by infinite compassion to us and to all other sentient beings, can directly guide and save us is through the conventional guru, this ordinary aspect. This aspect has manifested exactly according to the present state of our mind, which is impure. It is *only* from this aspect that we can receive guidance. Even though there have been so many lineage lamas in the past, we didn't have the karma to see and receive direct guidance from them. Even though there are numberless aspects of buddhas, they can't give us direct guidance because we can't see them. The only one left from whom we can receive direct guidance is this ordinary aspect, the conventional guru.

The absolute guru, by manifesting in or through this ordinary aspect, then directly guides us and saves us from suffering, from the sufferings of the lower realms and of samsara. The way this is done is by enabling us to abandon the negative karmas of killing, stealing, sexual misconduct, and so forth. Starting by abandoning these negative karmas, we are then able to gradually actualize the path, removing first the disturbing-thought obscurations and next the subtle obscurations. It brings us to enlightenment by causing us to actualize the path. The guru reveals the teachings, shows you the path, and from your own side you do the practices of listening, reflecting, and meditating. By actualizing the path and ceasing the disturbing-thought obscurations, which liberates you totally from the oceans of samsaric suffering, you are brought to liberation. Then, by actualizing the Mahayana path and ceasing even the subtle defilements, you are brought to enlightenment.

This just happened because I mentioned that you yourself become the guru-deity and that you have to realize there's no separation between the guru and the deity. That's similar to saying that you have to realize there's no separation between your guru and buddha. Because this topic came up, I just expanded on it a little. But this understanding is the very point of guru yoga, of guru devotion. This is the very heart; this is what we have to discover, to realize.

The absolute guru manifests in all the deities. With this realization you don't see any difference between Maitreya Buddha and the guru or between Tara and the guru. You don't see any separation between Manjushri and the guru. And it is the same with all the rest. It's all one being. No matter how many different aspects there are, all the buddhas, in reality, are one. Why are there so many different aspects? Because sentient beings have different karma. However, in reality, they're all one, and that one is the guru, the absolute guru.

Colophon

Excerpted from a teaching given by Kyabje Zopa Rinpoche at Root Institute, Bodhgaya, India on December 29, 2006. Transcribed and edited by Ven. Ailsa Cameron; published in *Roots of Wisdom*, the Root Institute newsletter. The whole teaching may be heard and read on line at LamaYeshe.com, Bodhgaya Teachings 2006, Day 4.

The Essential Advice of the Kadam Scriptures: A Fine Vase of Nectar

Chapter One

Making Requests to the Gurus and Relying on a Holy Spiritual Friend

Namo Guru Munindraya

Boundless leader, in the midst of all the constellations
Your share of marvelous courage is fully complete
And you are exceptionally beautified by the signs of compassion;
To you, unrivalled teacher possessing white [aura of] light, I bow.

Although we are followers of the supreme Teacher,
Due to our mind's eye being closed we cannot see the exalted
    body of the signs and exemplifications,
And due to the legs of our morality having degenerated we are
    unable to walk;
Out of your compassion please take care of us wretched ones.

Host of gurus of the lineage of vast conduct—
The conquerors' regent, Mipham;
The Dharma lords, Asanga and your brother;

The two Vimuktisenas, and the rest—
Please bless my mental continuum.

Host of gurus of the lineage of profound view—
Manjushri, who epitomizes the wisdom of the conquerors,
Arya Nagarjuna, Chandrakirti and the others—
Please bestow the excellent path of the middle way upon me.

Supreme gurus of the lineage of blessings—
The refuge lord Vajradhara and the Lord of Secrets,
Saraha, Tilopa, Naropa and so on—
Please bless my mental continuum.

You reached the end of the ocean-like conduct of the conquerors'
    children
Through upholding well the supreme mind, the germination
    of the conquerors,
In the presence of the conqueror Ratnagarbha:
To you, the conqueror Vimala, I make requests.

You satisfied all the fortunate Mahayanists without exception
Of India and Tibet through adopting the Mahayana nectar—
The quintessence of the ocean of Mahayana scriptures:
To you trailblazers of the Mahayana, I bow.

Due to your deeds resembling those of a second Lord of the Munis
For the sake of spreading the doctrine of the Muni throughout
    India and Tibet.

You are matchless in upholding the Muni's doctrine:

To you lamps for Munindra's teachings, I bow.

In particular, you nurture the wretched migrating beings

Of the northern direction with the nectar of the precious mind,

You of great heroic mind prophesied by the Conqueror:

At the feet of Dipamkara, I make requests.

Out of intolerable mercy for the utterly confused migrating beings

Of this country surrounded by brilliantly white snow mountains,

All the infinite conquerors along with their spiritual children

    without exception

Incarnated as an infant boy of shining crystal: to you, I bow.

You are the compassionate protector with special mercy

For the migrating beings of the northern direction

Who could not be subdued even by the compassionate peerless

    Teacher:

To you, venerable holder of a white lotus, I make requests.

You called "the sole source of the ocean of conquerors,"

Upon whose strength all the well-being and happiness without

    exception

Of the migrating beings pervading space entirely depends,

Are praised by all the conquerors: to you, [Dromtönpa], I bow.

Through inviting the glorious protector Dipamkara

By emanating inconceivable skillful means,

You dispelled the darkness obscuring Tibet:

At your feet, spiritual friend and teacher, I make requests.

You accomplished the strength of an ocean of great wave-like
    prayers,

For upholding the oral lineage of the profound and secret
    biographies

Of Dipamkara and the Source of Conquerors, [Dromtönpa]:

At your feet, Legpe Sherab (Excellent Wisdom), I make requests.

You satiated all the fortunate ones with the nectar of your vast
    conduct

Through the thousand-petaled lotus of your precious mind
    having blossomed

In the manner of correctly generating completely pure definite
    emergence:

To you, Rinchen Sel (Luminous Jewel), I make requests.

Having set the best of wishfulfilling jewels, the Kadam oral lineage,

On the tip of the victory banner of excellent practice,

You spontaneously enacted the two purposes of self and others:

At your feet, Zhönnu Gyeltsen (Youthful Victory Banner), I make
    requests.

Due to having accomplished the force of familiarization in
    many lifetimes,

In your youth you were blessed by the special deities,

Thereby becoming a treasure of instructions:
To you, Chen-nga Tsültrim Bar (Blazing Morality), I make requests.

The brilliance of your exalted knowledge of all the scriptures
    shone forth,
You destroyed the view of self with the vajra of equalizing and
    exchanging self and others,
And trained in cherishing others more than yourselves:
To you Kadam lamas, Chekawa and the rest, I make requests.

You are renowned in the lands of the boundless ten directions
As "the courageous conquerors' child" among all the merciful
    children of the conquerors;
Although you have thoroughly completed all good qualities,
Without concern you forsake your body and life in order to seek
    those very qualities;
Although you have fully attained the state of a conqueror,
You show the excellent and unmistaken path to migrating beings
In this degenerate time in the manner of a youthful conquerors'
    child;
To you, compassionate Jamgön, thoroughly renowned as
    resembling a second Lord of the Munis in spreading the
    teachings of Munindra, from my heart I bow.

You condensed without exception all the [Buddha's] words
And the treatises that comment on their intention into stages
    of practice

For a single fortunate being, and then expounded them;
To you, kind lama, I make requests. Please bless my continuum.

Please bless me to be able to rely properly upon
A virtuous spiritual friend who shows the excellent and
    unmistaken path,
The one upon whose force all the excellent collections
Of existence and peace without exception entirely depend.

Since it is necessary to examine whether or not you are able
    to trust
Even your escort when going to a dangerous place for a single day,
How can anyone at all be suitable to show
The path that progresses to the essence of enlightenment?

With regard to that, the Conqueror taught the qualifications of
A guru who shows the path in many sutras and tantras.
Having examined him well with an unbiased mind,
Rely on a spiritual friend who possesses the ten good qualities.

Through excellently thinking of
A qualified virtuous spiritual friend as the nature
That encompasses all the conquerors without exception,
Develop genuine devotion for him at all times and
Strive to please him by practicing in accordance with his
    instructions.

Just as you would dispose of spit as soon as it is seen,

Reject the boastful charlatans who deceive those with faith

By mixing the Dharma with various types of non-Dharma,

And do not be influenced by them even in a dream.

Do not abandon, even for the sake of your life, the holy spiritual
    friend

Who guides you on the path that delights the conquerors.

Through pleasing him with the three ways of pleasing,

Culminate the pure complete liberation of the Kadampas.

Among the quintessential practices of the essential advice that
    was expounded to the Dharma king Drom[tönpa] by the one
    divine, glorious, great lord Dipamkara, after he had completely
    condensed the essential meaning of the scriptures included
    in the three baskets and the four tantra classes, as well as their
    commentaries, this section—the definite importance of initially
    making requests to the gurus who possess the three lineages
    and properly relying on a holy spiritual friend, the root of all
    excellent collections—is the first chapter.

Colophon

This is the first chapter of Kachen Yeshe Gyaltsen's *The Essential Advice of the Kadam Scriptures: A Fine Vase of Nectar*, translated by Joan Nicell (Getsulma Tenzin Chöden) with the help of Geshe Jampa Gyatso at Istituto Lama Tzong Khapa, Pomaia, Italy, August 2007. The whole text is translated in *The Book of Kadam*, pp. 529–558.

Wendy Cook

Rinpoche at the Root Institute prayer wheel

··· Glossary ···

(Skt = Sanskrit; Tib = Tibetan)

Abhisamayalamkara (Skt). *Ornament for Clear Realizations*, by Maitreya; a philosophical text studied in Tibetan monasteries.

aggregates. The association of body and mind; a person comprises five aggregates: form, feeling, recognition, compositional factors and consciousness.

Amdo. The northeastern region of Tibet that borders on China.

anger. A disturbing thought that exaggerates the negative qualities of an object and wishes to harm it; one of the six root delusions.

arhat (Skt). Literally, foe destroyer. A being, who, having ceased his or her karma and delusions, is completely free from all suffering and its causes and has achieved liberation from cyclic existence.

Aryadeva. The chief disciple of Nagarjuna and a leading proponent of the Prasangika Madhyamaka school of Buddhist tenets.

Asanga. The fourth-century Indian master who received directly from Maitreya Buddha the extensive, or method, lineage of Shakyamuni Buddha's teachings.

asura (Skt). Or demigod. A being in the god realms who enjoys greater comfort and pleasure than human beings, but who suffers from jealousy and quarreling.

attachment. A disturbing thought that exaggerates the positive qualities of an object and wishes to possess it; one of the six root delusions.

attachment-scattering thought. An excited mind that is distracted from the object of meditation by objects of attachment; one of the interferences to the attainment of calm abiding.

bhumi (Skt). See *grounds and paths*.

Bodhgaya. A small town in the state of Bihar in north India that is built around the site where Shakyamuni Buddha became enlightened.

bodhicitta (Skt). The altruistic determination to achieve full enlightenment in order to free all sentient beings from suffering and its causes and bring them to enlightenment.

bodhisattva (Skt). One who possesses bodhicitta.

Boudhanath. A village just outside Kathmandu that is built around the Boudhanath Stupa, a famous Buddhist pilgrimage site.

buddha (Skt). A fully enlightened being. One who has purified all obscurations of the mind and perfected all good qualities. See also *enlightenment, Shakyamuni Buddha*.

buddha-nature. Refers to the emptiness, or ultimate nature, of the mind. Because of this nature, every sentient being possesses the potential to become fully enlightened.

Buxa Duar. A small village in West Bengal in eastern India on the Bhutanese border at the foot of the British-built Buxa Fort, where most of the Tibetan monks who escaped to India in 1959 were accommodated.

calm abiding. See *shamatha*.

Chenrezig (Tib; Skt: *Avalokiteshvara*). The Buddha of Compassion. The male meditational deity that embodies the compassion of all the buddhas. The Dalai Lamas are said to be emanations of this deity.

Chöden Rinpoche (b. 1933). An ascetic, learned Gelugpa lama who meditated in a small room in Lhasa for nineteen years after the Chinese occupation; a guru of Lama Zopa Rinpoche.

Chogye Trichen Rinpoche (1919–2007). A highly learned and attained lama who was head of the Tsarpa branch of the Sakya tradition; a guru of Lama Zopa Rinpoche.

chu-len (Tib). Or taking the essence. A practice in which food is replaced by pills made from minerals or flowers as an aid to concentration.

compassion. The sincere wish that others be free from suffering and its causes.

Compassion Buddha. See *Chenrezig.*

completion stage. The more advanced of the two stages of Highest Yoga Tantra.

consciousness. See *mind.*

daka (Skt). The male equivalent of a dakini.

dakini (Skt). Literally, sky-goer; a female being with tantric realizations of the generation or completion stages.

Dakpa Khachö (Tib; Skt: *Kechara*). The pure land of Vajrayogini.

Dagpo Rinpoche. Jampel Lhundrup. Pabongka Rinpoche's root guru for lam-rim teachings; author of the Jorchö text *A Necklace for the Fortunate*; his reincarnation has lived in France for many years.

Dalai Lama, His Holiness the Fourteenth (b. 1935). Gyalwa Tenzin Gyatso. Revered spiritual leader of the Tibetan people and tireless worker for world peace; winner of the Nobel Peace Prize in 1989; a guru of Lama Zopa Rinpoche.

deity (Tib: *yidam*). The form of a buddha used as an object of meditation in tantric practices.

delusions. The disturbing, negative thoughts that are the cause of suffering. The three root delusions are ignorance, anger and attachment.

dependent arising. The way that the self and phenomena exist conventionally as relative and interdependent. They come into existence in dependence upon (1) causes and conditions, (2) their parts and, most subtly, (3) the mind imputing, or labeling, them.

desire. See *attachment.*

desire realm. One of the three realms of samsara, comprising the hell beings, hungry ghosts, animals, humans, asuras and the six lower classes of suras; beings in this realm are preoccupied with desire for objects of the six senses.

deva (Skt). A god dwelling in a state with much comfort and pleasure in the desire, form or formless realms.

Deva's Son (Skt: *devaputramara*). One of the four types of maras; interferes with meditation by increasing desire for sensual pleasures.

Dharma (Skt). In general, spiritual practice; specifically, the teachings of Buddha, which protect from suffering and lead to liberation and full enlightenment.

dharmakaya (Skt). Truth body; the blissful omniscient mind of a buddha.

Dharma protectors. Beings, some worldly and others enlightened, who protect Dharma teachings and practitioners.

disturbing thoughts. See *delusions.*

disturbing-thought obscurations (Tib: *nyön-drib*). The delusions, which obstruct the attainment of liberation.

Domo Geshe Rinpoche (d. 1936). A famous ascetic meditator in his early life who later established monastic communities in the Tibet-Nepal border area and in Darjeeling; the guru of Lama Govinda, author of *The Way of the White Clouds.*

Dragpa Gyaltsen (1147–1216). A great scholar and early teacher of the Sakya school; uncle and guru of Sakya Pandita.

Drepung Monastery. The largest of the three major Gelugpa monasteries; founded near Lhasa by one of Lama Tsongkhapa's disciples. Now reestablished in exile in south India.

Dromtönpa (1005–64). Lama Atisha's heart disciple and chief translator in Tibet; propagator of the Kadampa tradition.

du-ra (Tib). The subject, preliminary to debating, in which basic terms and definitions are explained.

eight freedoms. The eight states from which a perfect human rebirth is free: being born as a hell-being, hungry ghost, animal, long-life god or barbarian, or in a dark age when no buddha has descended; holding wrong views; or being born with defective mental or physical faculties.

Eight Mahayana Precepts. One-day vows to abandon killing; stealing; lying; sexual contact; intoxicants; high seats; eating at the wrong time; and singing, dancing and wearing perfumes and jewelry.

eight worldly dharmas. The worldly concerns that generally motivate the actions of ordinary beings: being happy when given gifts and unhappy when not given them; wanting to be happy and not wanting to be unhappy; wanting praise and not wanting criticism; wanting a good reputation and not wanting a bad reputation.

emptiness (Skt: *shunyata*). The absence, or lack, of true existence. Ultimately, every phenomenon is empty of existing truly, or from its own side, or independently. (See also *merely labeled*.)

enlightenment. Full awakening; buddhahood. The ultimate goal of Mahayana Buddhist practice, attained when all faults have been removed from the mind and all realizations completed; a state characterized by the perfection of compassion, wisdom and power.

form realm. The second of samsara's three realms, with seventeen classes of gods.

formless realm. The highest of samsara's three realms, with four classes of gods involved in formless meditation.

Ganden Monastery. The first of the three great Gelugpa monastic universities near Lhasa, founded in 1409 by Lama Tsongkhapa. It was badly damaged in the 1960s and has now been reestablished in exile in south India.

Gen Jampa Wangdu (d. 1984). As ascetic meditator who was a close friend of Lama Yeshe and a guru of Lama Zopa Rinpoche.

geshe (Tib). Literally, spiritual friend. The title conferred on those who have completed extensive studies and examinations at Gelugpa monastic universities, but also given to the early Kadampa masters.

Geshe Chekawa (1101–75). The Kadampa geshe who was inspired by Geshe Langri Tangpa's *Eight Verses of Thought Transformation* and later composed the famous thought transformation text *Seven-Point Mind Training.*

Geshe Doga (b. 1935). Resident teacher for more than twenty-five years at Tara Institute, the FPMT center in Melbourne, Australia.

Geshe Dölpa (1059–1131). Sherab Gyatso; a disciple of Geshe Potowa and compiler of *Blue Manual.*

Geshe Kharak Gomchung (late 11th century). A disciple of Gönpawa Wangchuk Gyaltsen; the dedicated meditator who could not even find time to cut the thorn bush outside his meditation room.

Geshe Namgyal Wangchen (b. 1934). Educated at Drepung Monastery in Tibet, after serving as the resident teacher at Jamyang Buddhist Centre, London, for many years, Geshe Wangchen is now a respected teacher at the reestablished Drepung Monastery in south India.

Geshe Potowa (1031–1105). Also known as Potowa Rinchen Sel. Entered Reting Monastery in 1058 and became its abbot for a short time; one of the three great disciples of Dromtönpa; patriarch of the Kadampa Treatise lineage.

Geshe Rabten (1920–86). The learned Gelugpa lama who was a religious assistant to His Holiness the Dalai Lama before moving to Switzerland in 1975; a guru of Lama Yeshe and Lama Zopa Rinpoche.

Geshe Sopa Rinpoche (b. 1923). An eminent Buddhist scholar based at Deer Park in Wisconsin, U.S.A. and guru of both Lama Yeshe and Lama Zopa Rinpoche

god. See *deva.*

gompa (Tib). Usually refers to the main meditation hall, or temple, within a monastery.

graduated path to enlightenment. See *lam-rim.*

grounds and paths. There are five paths and eight bodhisattva grounds (Skt: *bhumi*) in the Mahayana path to full enlightenment.

Gungtang Rinpoche (1762–1823). Könchog Tenpai Drönme. A disciple of the first incarnation of the great Jamyang Shepa; known for his eloquent spiritual poetry and philosophical works.

guru (Skt; Tib: *lama*). Literally, heavy, as in heavy with Dharma knowledge. A spiritual teacher, master.

guru devotion. The sutra or tantra practice of seeing the guru as a buddha then devoting to him with thought and action.

Guru Puja (Tib: *Lama Chöpa*). A special Highest Yoga Tantra guru yoga practice composed by Panchen Losang Chökyi Gyaltsen.

guru yoga (Skt). The tantric practice of meditating on the guru and deity as inseparably one, then merging this guru-deity with one's own mind; the various sadhanas that incorporate these meditations.

Gyalwa Götsangpa (1189–1258). Also known as Gönpo Dorje. A Kagyü master who was a disciple of Tsangpa Gyare.

Gyalwa Gyatso (Tib). A semi-wrathful Highest Yoga Tantra aspect of Chenrezig.

happy transmigratory being. A samsaric being in the realms of suras, asuras or humans.

hell. The samsaric realm with the greatest physical suffering. There are eight hot hells, eight cold hells and four neighboring hells.

Highest Yoga Tantra (Skt: *maha-anuttara yoga tantra*). The fourth and supreme of the four classes of tantra, which mainly emphasizes internal activities.

Hinayana (Skt). Literally, Lesser Vehicle. The path of the arhats, the goal of which is nirvana, or personal liberation from samsara.

holy signs and exemplifications. The thirty-two holy signs and eighty exemplifications are unique physical characteristics of a buddha.

ignorance. A mental factor that obscures the mind from seeing the way in which things exist in reality. There are basically two types of ignorance: ignorance of karma and ignorance that holds the concept of true existence, the fundamental delusion from which all other delusions arise.

impermanence. The gross and subtle levels of the transience of phenomena.

imprints. The seeds, or potentials, left on the mind by positive or negative actions of body, speech and mind.

intermediate state (Tib: *bardo*). The state between death and rebirth, lasting anywhere from a moment to forty-nine days.

Jorchö (Tib). Six preparatory practices that prepare the mind for lam-rim meditation.

Kachen Yeshe Gyaltsen (1713–93). Tsechokling Rinpoche. A recent lineage lama of mahamudra; tutor of the Ninth Dalai Lama; founded Tsechok Ling Monastery in Lhasa.

Kadampa geshe. A practitioner of the Buddhist tradition that originated in Tibet in the eleventh century with the teachings of Lama Atisha. Kadampa geshes are renowned for their practice of thought transformation.

Kangyur (Tib). The part of the Tibetan Buddhist canon that contains the discourses of Shakyamuni Buddha.

karma (Skt). Literally, action. The working of cause and effect, whereby positive actions produce happiness and negative actions produce suffering.

Kham. The area of Tibet east of Lhasa and west of Amdo.

Khunu Lama Tenzin Gyaltsen (1894–1977). A renowned bodhisattva born in northern Inda; a scholar of Sanskrit who studied in Tibet with many teachers from different schools; a guru of Lama Zopa Rinpoche.

Khyongla Rato Rinpoche (b. 1923). In 1975 founded Tibet Center, the oldest Tibetan Buddhist center in New York City; a guru of Lama Zopa Rinpoche.

Kirti Tsenshab Rinpoche (1926–2006). A highly attained and learned ascetic yogi who lived in Dharamsala, India; one of Lama Zopa Rinpoche's gurus.

Konchog Gyaltsen (1388–1469). Co-compiler of *Mind Training: The Great Collection*; holder of the Ngor throne of the Sakya school.

Kopan Monastery. The monastery near Boudhanath in the Kathmandu valley, Nepal founded by Lama Yeshe and Lama Zopa Rinpoche.

Krishnacharya (Tib: *Nagpo Chöpa*). Also known as Krishnachari and Kanhapa; one of the eight-four siddhas.

Kshitigarbha (Skt). One of the eight bodhisattvas.

Kusali (Skt). A name given to a hidden practitioner.

lama (Tib). See *guru.*

Lama Atisha (982–1054). The renowned Indian master who went to Tibet in 1042 to help in the revival of Buddhism and established the Kadam tradition. His text *Lamp of the Path* was the first lam-rim text.

Lama Ösel (b. 1985). The Spanish reincarnation of Lama Yeshe.

Lama Tsongkhapa (1357–1419). The revered teacher and accomplished practitioner who founded the Gelug order of Tibetan Buddhism. An emanation of Manjushri, Buddha of Wisdom.

Lama Yeshe (1935–84). Born and educated in Tibet, he fled to India, where he met his chief disciple, Lama Zopa Rinpoche. They began teaching Westerners at Kopan Monastery in 1969 and founded the FPMT (Foundation for the Preservation of the Mahayana Tradition) in 1975.

lam-rim (Tib). The graduated path to enlightenment. A presentation of Shakyamuni Buddha's teachings as step-by-step training for a disciple to achieve enlightenment.

Langri Tangpa (1054–1123). Dorje Senge. Author of the famous *Eight Verses of Thought Transformation*.

Lati Rinpoche (b. 1922). A respected Gelugpa lama and an ex-abbot of Ganden Shartse Monastery.

Lawudo. The cave in the Solu Khumbu region of Nepal where the Lawudo Lama meditated for more than twenty years. Lama Zopa Rinpoche is recognized as the reincarnation of the Lawudo Lama.

liberation (Skt: *nirvana*). The state of complete freedom from samsara; the goal of a practitioner seeking their own freedom from suffering.

lineage lama. A spiritual teacher who is in the line of direct guru-disciple transmission of teachings, from Buddha to the teachers of the present day.

Losang Dragpa. See *Lama Tsongkhapa*.

loving kindness. The wish for others to have happiness and its causes.

lower realms. The three realms of cycle existence with the most suffering: the hell, hungry ghost and animal realms.

lung (Tib). Literally, wind. The state in which the winds within the body are unbalanced or blocked, thus causing various illnesses. Can also refer to an oral transmission.

Madhyamaka (Skt). The Middle Way School, a philosophical system founded by Nagarjuna, based on the *Perfection of Wisdom Sutras* of Shakyamuni Buddha, and considered to be the supreme presentation of Buddha's teachings on emptiness.

Mahayana (Skt). Literally, Great Vehicle. The path of the bodhisattvas, those seeking enlightenment in order to enlighten all other beings.

Maitreya Buddha (Skt; Tib: *Jampa*). The Loving One. The next buddha, after Shakyamuni, and the fifth of the thousand buddhas of this present world age.

mala (Skt). A rosary of beads for counting mantras.

Manjugosha. See *Manjushri*.

Manjushri (Skt). A male meditational deity who embodies the wisdom of all the buddhas.

mantra (Skt). Literally, mind protection. Sanskrit syllables usually recited in conjunction with the practice of a particular meditational deity and embodying the qualities of that deity.

maras (Skt). Internal interferences, such as those from karma and delusions, or external interferences, such as those from spirits or devas.

Marpa (1012–96). A great Tibetan Buddhist translator and yogi; a founding figure of the Kagyü tradition and root guru of Milarepa.

Medicine Buddha. An Action Tantra meditational deity practiced for healing and general success.

meditation. Familiarization of the mind with a virtuous object. There are two main types of meditation: analytical and concentration, or fixed.

merely labeled. The subtlest meaning of dependent arising; every phenomenon exists relatively, or conventionally, as a mere label, merely imputed by the mind.

merit. The positive energy accumulated in the mind as a result of virtuous actions of body, speech and mind. The principal cause of happiness.

merit field. Or field of accumulation. The visualized or actual holy beings in relation to whom one accumulates merit by going for refuge, making offerings and so forth and to whom one prays or makes requests for special purposes.

migtsema (Tib). A verse of praise recited during the practice of Lama Tsongkhapa Guru Yoga.

Milarepa (1040–1123). A great Tibetan yogi and poet famed for his impeccable relationship with his guru, Marpa, his asceticism and his songs of realization. A founding figure of the Kagyü tradition.

mind. Synonymous with consciousness. Defined as "that which is clear and knowing"; a formless entity that has the ability to perceive objects.

Mount Meru. The center of the universe in Buddhist cosmology.

nagas (Skt). Snake-like beings of the animal realm who live in or near bodies of water.

Nagarjuna. The great second-century Indian philosopher and tantric adept who propounded the Madhyamaka philosophy of emptiness.

negative karma. The negative thoughts and actions that result in suffering.

nonvirtuous action. See *negative karma.*

Nyingmapas (Tib). Followers of the oldest of the four traditions of Tibetan Buddhism, which traces its teachings back to Padmasambhava.

object to be refuted (Tib: *gak-cha*). The true, or inherent, existence of the self and other phenomena.

obscurations. The negative imprints left on the mind by negative karma and delusions, which obscure the mind.

OM MANI PADME HUM (Skt). The *mani;* the mantra of Chenrezig, Buddha of Compassion.

oral transmission (Tib: *lung*). The verbal transmission of a teaching, meditation practice or mantra from guru to disciple, the guru having received the transmission in an unbroken lineage from the original source.

Pabongka Dechen Nyingpo (1871–1941). An influential and charismatic Gelugpa lama, Pabongka Rinpoche was the root guru of His Holiness the Fourteenth Dalai Lama's tutors. He also gave the teachings compiled in *Liberation in the Palm of Your Hand.*

Padmasambhava. The eighth-century Indian tantric master mainly responsible for the establishment of Buddhism in Tibet, revered by all Tibetan Buddhists, but especially by Nyingmapas.

Panchen Rinpoche. Lineage representing incarnations of Amitabha Buddha; the Panchen Lama and the Dalai Lama re the two highest spiritual leaders of Tibet.

paramitas (Skt). Or perfections. The practices of a bodhisattva. On the basis of bodhicitta, a bodhisattva practices the six paramitas: generosity, morality, patience, enthusiastic perseverance, concentration and wisdom.

Paramitayana (Skt). Literally, Perfection Vehicle. The bodhisattva vehicle; a section of the Mahayana sutra teachings; one of the two forms of Mahayana, the other being Tantrayana.

path of meditation. The fourth of the five paths leading to buddhahood.

path of seeing. The third of the five paths to buddhahood; attained with the direct perception of emptiness.

perfect human rebirth. The rare human state, qualified by eight freedoms and ten richnesses, which is the ideal condition for practicing Dharma and attaining enlightenment.

pervasive compounding suffering. The most subtle of the three types of suffering, it refers to the nature of the five aggregates, which are contaminated by karma and delusions.

Prajnaparamita (Skt). The Perfection of Wisdom. The second teaching, or turning of the wheel of Shakyamuni Buddha, in which the wisdom of emptiness and the path of the bodhisattva are explained.

Prasangika (Skt). The Middle Way Consequence School; considered to be the highest of all Buddhist philosophical tenets.

pratimoksha (Skt). The vows of individual liberation taken by monks, nuns and lay people.

preliminary practices. The practices that prepare the mind for successful tantric meditation by removing hindrances and accumulating merit.

preta (Skt). Or hungry ghost. One of the six classes of samsaric beings, pretas experience the greatest sufferings of hunger and thirst.

prostrations. Paying respect with body, speech and mind to gurus, buddhas, deities and other holy objects; one of the tantric preliminary practices.

protector. A worldly or enlightened being who protects Buddhism and its practitioners.

puja (Skt). Literally, offering; a religious ceremony.

Rachevsky, Zina (1931–73). Lama Yeshe's and Lama Zopa Rinpoche's first Western student, she helped them to establish Kopan Monastery and died in retreat in Solu Khumbu.

refuge. The heartfelt reliance upon Buddha, Dharma and Sangha for guidance on the path to enlightenment.

Rinpoche (Tib). Literally, precious one. Generally, a title given to a lama who has intentionally taken rebirth in a human body to continue helping others. A respectful title for one's own lama.

Sakya (Tib). One of the four principal traditions of Tibetan Buddhism, it was founded in the eleventh century by Khön Konchog Gyälpo (1034–1102).

Sakya Pandita (1182–1251). The title of Kunga Gyaltsen, a master of the Sakya tradition, who spread Tibetan Buddhism in Mongolia and China.

Samantabhadra. A bodhisattva renowned for his heroic aspiration and extensive offerings.

samsara (Skt). Cyclic existence; the recurring cycle of death and rebirth within one or other of the six realms. It also refers to the contaminated aggregates of a sentient being.

Sangha (Skt). The third object of refuge; absolute Sangha are those who have directly realized emptiness; relative Sangha are ordained monks and nuns.

self-cherishing. The self-centered attitude of considering one's own happiness to be more important than that of others; the main obstacle to the realization of bodhicitta.

sentient being. Any unenlightened being; any being whose mind is not completely free of ignorance.

Sera Monastery. One of three great Gelugpa monasteries near Lhasa, now also established in exile in south India. It has two colleges, Sera Je, with which Lama Zopa Rinpoche is connected, and Sera Me.

Serkong Dorje Chang (1920–79). The great twentieth century yogi who lived for many years at the holy place of Swayambhunath in Nepal; a guru of Lama Zopa Rinpoche.

Shakyamuni Buddha (563–483 BCE). The founder of the present Buddhadharma. Fourth of the one thousand buddhas of this present world age, he was born a prince of the Shakya clan in north India and taught the sutra and tantra paths to liberation and full enlightenment.

shamatha (Skt; Tib: *shi-nä*). Calm abiding; a state of concentration in which the mind is able to abide steadily, without effort and for as long as desired, on an object of meditation.

Shantideva (685–763). The great Indian bodhisattva who wrote *A Guide to the Bodhisattva's Way of Life,* one of the essential Mahayana texts.

Shariputra. An arhat renowned for his wisdom; one of Shakyamuni Buddha's two chief disciples.

Sherpas. The people of Solu Khumbu in Nepal; originally from Kham in Tibet.

siddhi (Skt). Attainment. There are eight ordinary attainments and one superior attainment, buddhahood.

single-pointed concentration. The ability to focus effortlessly and for as long as one wishes on an object of meditation.

sinking thought. Or mental dullness; one of the interferences to attaining calm abiding.

Six Yogas of Naropa. A set of completion state tantric practices, including tummo meditation.

Solu Khumbu. The area in north-eastern Nepal, bordering Tibet, where Lama Zopa Rinpoche was born; populated by Sherpas.

stupa (Skt). A reliquary symbolic of a buddha's mind.

subtle dependent arising. See *merely labeled.*

subtle obscurations (Tib: *she-drib*). The subtle defilements of the mind that obstruct the attainment of enlightenment.

suffering of change. What is normally regarded as pleasure, which because of its transitory nature sooner or later turns into suffering.

suffering of pain. The commonly recognized suffering experiences of pain, discomfort and unhappiness.

sura (Skt). A being in the god realm who enjoys the highest pleasures to be found in cyclic existence.

Svatantrika (Skt). The Autonomous Middle Way school; one of the two Madhyamaka schools of Buddhist tenets.

tantra (Skt). The secret teachings of the Buddha; a scriptural text and the teachings and practices it contains.

Tara (Skt; Tib: *Drolma*). A female meditational deity who embodies the enlightened activity of all the buddhas; one of the four major deities practiced by the Kadampas.

Tashi Lhunpo Monastery. The Panchen Lamas' monastery in Shigatse in

Tibet; built by the First Dalai Lama, Gyalwa Gendun Drub; now reestablished in exile in south India.

tathagata (Skt). Literally, Thus Gone; an epithet of a buddha.

ten nonvirtuous actions. The three nonvirtues of body are killing, stealing and sexual misconduct; the four nonvirtues of speech are lying, slander, harsh speech and gossip; the three nonvirtues of mind are covetousness, ill will and wrong views.

ten richnesses. The ten qualities that characterize a perfect human rebirth: being born as a human being, in a Dharma country and with perfect mental and physical faculties; being free of the five uninterrupted negative karmas; having faith in Buddha's teachings; being born when a buddha has descended, when the teachings are still alive, when there are still followers of the teachings and having the necessary conditions to practice Dharma.

Tengyur (Tib). The part of the Tibetan Buddhist canon that contains commentaries by Indian pandits on the discourses of Shakyamuni Buddha.

Tenzin Gyatso. See *Dalai Lama, His Holiness the Fourteenth.*

Thirty-five Buddhas. Used in the practice of confessing and purifying negative karmas, the group of thirty-five buddhas visualized while reciting *The Sutra of the Three Heaps* and performing prostrations.

Thirty-three realm. A god realm in the desire realm; the abode of Indra.

thought transformation (Tib: *lo-jong*). A powerful approach to the development of bodhicitta, in which the mind is trained to use all situations, both happy and unhappy, as a means to destroy self-cherishing and self-grasping.

three great meanings. The happiness of future lives, liberation and enlightenment.

Trijang Rinpoche (1901–81). The later Junior Tutor of His Holiness the Fourteenth Dalai Lama and root guru of Lama Yeshe and Lama Zopa Rinpoche.

Triple Gem. The objects of Buddhist refuge: Buddha, Dharma and Sangha.

true existence. The type of concrete, real existence from its own side that everything appears to possess; in fact, everything is empty of true existence.

tsa-tsa (Tib). A print of a buddha's image made in clay or plaster from a carved mold.

Tushita (Skt). The Joyous Land. The pure land of the thousand buddhas of this eon, where the future buddha, Maitreya, and Lama Tsongkhapa reside.

twenty-four holy places. Sacred sites in India and Nepal associated especially with Chakrasamvara; also Hindu holy sites.

upper realms. The human and god realms.

Vaibhashika (Skt). The Great Exposition school, one of the two principal Hinayana schools of Buddhist tenets.

Vajrasattva (Skt; Tib: *Dorje Sempa*). A male tantric deity used especially for purification.

Vajravarahi (Skt; Tib: *Dorje Phagmo*). An aspect of Vajrayogini.

Vajrayogini (Skt; Tib: Dorje Näljorma). A semi-wrathful female tantric deity.

virtue. Positive karma; that which results in happiness.

wisdom mother. A tantric consort.

Yamantaka (Skt). Or Vajrabhairava. The wrathful male deity that is the Highest Yoga Tantra aspect of Manjushri.

yidam (Tib). See deity.

yogi (Skt). A highly realized meditator.

···Bibliography···

Aryadeva. *Aryadeva's Four Hundred Stanzas on the Middle Way: With Commentary by Gyel-tsap.* Translated by Ruth Sonam with additional commentary by Geshe Sonam Rinchen. Ithaca: Snow Lion Publications, 2007.

FPMT. *Essential Buddhist Prayers: An FPMT Prayer Book, Volume 1, Basic Prayers and Practices.* Portland: FPMT, Inc., 2006.

Govinda, Lama Anagarika. *The Way of the White Clouds: A Buddhist Pilgrim in Tibet.* London: Hutchinson, 1968.

Gyatso, Tenzin, the Fourteenth Dalai Lama. *Illuminating the Path to Enlightenment: A Commentary on Atisha Dipamkara Shrijnana's* A Lamp for the Path to Enlightenment *and Lama Je Tsong Khapa's* Lines of Experience. Translated by Geshe Thupten Jinpa. Edited by Rebecca McClen Novick, Thupten Jinpa and Nicholas Ribush. Boston: Lama Yeshe Wisdom Archive, 2002. On line at LamaYeshe.com.

————. *Opening the Eye of New Awareness.* Translated by Donald S. Lopez. Boston: Wisdom Publications, 1999.

————. *The Union of Bliss and Emptiness: Teachings on the Practice of Guru Yoga.* Translated by Thupten Jinpa. Ithaca: Snow Lion Publications, 2009.

Jinpa, Thupten (trans). *The Book of Kadam: The Core Texts.* Boston: Wisdom Publications, 2008.

————. *Mind Training: The Great Collection.* Compiled by Shönu Gyalchok and Könchok Gyaltsen. Boston: Wisdom Publications, 2006.

Kalsang, Lama Thubten et al (trans). *Atisha: A Biography of the Renowned Buddhist Sage.* Bangkok: The Social Science Association Press, 1974. On line at LamaYeshe.com.

Lati Rinbochay and Denma Lochö Rinbochay. *Meditative States in Tibetan Buddhism.* Translated by Leah Zahler and Jeffrey Hopkins. Boston: Wisdom Publications, 1997.

Nagarjuna. *Nagarjuna's Letter.* Translated by Geshe Lobsang Tharchin and Artemus B. Engle. Dharamsala: Library of Tibetan Works and Archives, 1979.

Pabongka Rinpoche. *Liberation in the Palm of Your Hand: A Concise Discourse on the Path to Enlightenment*. Edited by Trijang Rinpoche. Translated by Michael Richards. Boston: Wisdom Publications, 2006.

Rabten, Geshe. *The Essential Nectar: Meditations on the Buddhist Path*. Editing and verse translation by Martin Willson. Boston: Wisdom Publications, 1992.

——— and Geshe Ngawang Dhargyey. *Advice from a Spiritual Friend*. Translated by Brian Beresford. Boston: Wisdom Publications, 1996.

Ribush, Nicholas (ed). *Teachings from Tibet: Guidance from Great Lamas*. Boston: Lama Yeshe Wisdom Archive, 2005.

Shantideva. *A Guide to the Bodhisattva's Way of Life*. Translated by Stephen Batchelor. Dharamsala: Library of Tibetan Works and Archives, 1992.

———. *A Guide to the Bodhisattva Way of Life*. Translated by Vesna A. Wallace and B. Alan Wallace. Ithaca, New York: Snow Lion Publications, 1997.

Tsong-kha-pa, Lama. *The Great Treatise on the Stages of the Path to Enlightenment: Volume 3*. Translated by the Lamrim Chenmo Translation Committee. Ithaca: Snow Lion Publications, 2002.

———. *The Principal Teachings of Buddhism*. With a commentary by Pabongka Rinpoche. Translated by Geshe Lobsang Tharchin. Howell, New Jersey: Mahayana Sutra and Tantra Press, 1988.

Wangchen, Geshe Namgyal. *Step by Step: Basic Buddhist Meditations*. Boston: Wisdom Publications, 2009.

Zopa Rinpoche, Lama. *The Heart of the Path: Seeing the Guru as Buddha*. Edited by Ailsa Cameron. Boston, Lama Yeshe Wisdom Archive, 2009.

——— (comp and trans). *The Direct and Unmistaken Method*. Portland: FPMT, Inc., 2009.

SUGGESTED FURTHER READING

Dilgo Khyentse Rinpoche. *Enlightened Courage: An Explanation of Atisha's Seven Point Mind Training.* Translated by the Padmakara Translation Group. Ithaca: Snow Lion Publications, 1993.

Gomo Tulku. *Becoming a Child of the Buddhas: A Simple Clarification of the Root Verses of Seven-Point Mind Training.* Translated and edited by Joan Nicell. Boston: Wisdom Publications, 1997.

Pel, Namkha. *Mind Training Like the Rays of the Sun.* Translated by Brian Beresford and edited by Jeremy Russell. Dharamsala: Library of Tibetan Works and Archives, 1992.

Rinchen, Geshe Sonam. *Atisha's Lamp for the Path to Enlightenment.* Translated and edited by Ruth Sonam. Ithaca, New York: Snow Lion Publications, 1997.

———. *Eight Verses for Training the Mind.* Translated and edited by Ruth Sonam. Ithaca: New York, 2007.

———. *The Three Principal Aspects of the Path.* Translated and edited by Ruth Sonam. Ithaca, New York: Snow Lion Publications, 1999.

Shantideva. *The Way of the Bodhisattva: A Translation of the Bodhicharyavatara.* Translated by the Padmakara Translation Group. Boston: Shambhala Publications, 1997.

Sherbourne, Richard. S.J. *A Lamp for the Path and Commentary.* London: George Allen & Unwin, 1983.

Sopa, Geshe Lhundrub. *Peacock in a Poison Grove: Two Tibetan Mind Training Texts.* Edited by Michael Sweet and Leonard Zwilling. Boston: Wisdom Publications, 1997.

Thegchok, Geshe Jampa. *The Kindness of Others: A Commentary on the Seven-Point Mind Training.* Translated by Stephen Carlier and edited by Andy Wistreich, Linda Gatter and Nicholas Ribush. Boston: Lama Yeshe Wisdom Archive, 2006.

Thondup Rinpoche, Tulku (trans). *Enlightened Living: Teachings of Tibetan Buddhist Masters.* Edited by Harold Talbott. Kathmandu: Rangjung Yeshe Publications, 1997.

Wangmo, Jamyang. *The Lawudo Lama: Stories of Reincarnation from the Mount Everest Region.* Boston: Wisdom Publications, 2005.

Wangyal, Geshe (trans). *The Door of Liberation: Essential Teachings of the Tibetan Buddhist Tradition.* Boston: Wisdom Publications, 1995.

Zopa Rinpoche, Lama. *The Door to Satisfaction: The Heart Advice of a Tibetan Buddhist Master*. Edited by Ailsa Cameron and Robina Courtin. Boston: Wisdom Publications, 2001.

———. *Transforming Problems into Happiness*. Boston: Wisdom Publications, 2001.

LAMA YESHE WISDOM ARCHIVE

The LAMA YESHE WISDOM ARCHIVE (LYWA) is the collected works of Lama Thubten Yeshe and Lama Thubten Zopa Rinpoche. Lama Zopa Rinpoche, its spiritual director, founded the ARCHIVE in 1996.

Lama Yeshe and Lama Zopa Rinpoche began teaching at Kopan Monastery, Nepal, in 1970. Since then, their teachings have been recorded and transcribed. At present we have well over 10,000 hours of digital audio and some 70,000 pages of raw transcript. Many recordings, mostly teachings by Lama Zopa Rinpoche, remain to be transcribed, and as Rinpoche continues to teach, the number of recordings in the ARCHIVE increases accordingly. Most of our transcripts have been neither checked nor edited.

Here at the LYWA we are making every effort to organize the transcription of that which has not yet been transcribed, edit that which has not yet been edited, and generally do the many other tasks detailed below.

The work of the LAMA YESHE WISDOM ARCHIVE falls into two categories: archiving and dissemination.

Archiving requires managing the recordings of teachings by Lama Yeshe and Lama Zopa Rinpoche that have already been collected, collecting recordings of teachings given but not yet sent to the ARCHIVE, and collecting recordings of Lama Zopa's on-going teachings, talks, advice and so forth as he travels the world for the benefit of all. Incoming media are then catalogued and stored safely while being kept accessible for further work.

We organize the transcription of audio, add the transcripts to the already existent database of teachings, manage this database, have transcripts checked, and make transcripts available to editors or others doing research on or practicing these teachings.

Other archiving activities include working with video and photographs of the Lamas and digitizing ARCHIVE materials.

Dissemination involves making the Lamas' teachings available through various avenues including books for free distribution and sale, lightly edited transcripts, a monthly e-letter (see below), DVDs, articles in *Mandala* and other magazines and on our website. Irrespective of the medium we choose, the teachings require a significant amount of work to prepare them for distribution.

This is just a summary of what we do. The ARCHIVE was established with virtually no seed funding and has developed solely through the kindness of many people, some of whom we have mentioned at the front of this book and most of the others on our website. We sincerely thank them all.

Our further development similarly depends upon the generosity of those who see the benefit and necessity of this work, and we would be extremely grateful for your help. Thus we hereby appeal to you for your kind support. If you would like to make a contribution to help us with any of the above tasks or to sponsor books for free distribution, please contact us:

LAMA YESHE WISDOM ARCHIVE
PO Box 356, Weston, MA 02493, USA
Telephone (781) 259-4466; Fax (678) 868-4806
info@LamaYeshe.com
www.LamaYeshe.com

The LAMA YESHE WISDOM ARCHIVE is a 501(c)(3) tax-deductible, non-profit corporation dedicated to the welfare of all sentient beings and totally dependent upon your donations for its continued existence. Thank you so much for your support. You may contribute by mailing a check, bank draft or money order to our Weston address; by making a donation on our secure website; by mailing us your credit card number or phoning it in; or by transferring funds directly to our bank—ask us for details.

LAMA YESHE WISDOM ARCHIVE MEMBERSHIP

In order to raise the money we need to employ editors to make available the thousands of hours of teachings mentioned above, we have established a membership plan. Membership costs US$1,000 and its main benefit is that you will be helping make the Lamas' incredible teachings available to a worldwide audience. More direct and tangible benefits to you personally include free Lama Yeshe and Lama Zopa Rinpoche books from the AR-CHIVE and Wisdom Publications, a year's subscription to *Mandala*, a year of monthly pujas by the monks and nuns at Kopan Monastery with your personal dedication, and access to an exclusive members-only section of our website containing special, unpublished teachings currently unavailable to others. Please see www.LamaYeshe.com for more information.

MONTHLY E-LETTER

Each month we send out a free e-letter containing our latest news and a previously unpublished teaching by Lama Yeshe or Lama Zopa Rinpoche. To see nearly eighty back-issues or to subscribe with your email address, please go to our website.

THE FOUNDATION FOR THE PRESERVATION OF THE MAHAYANA TRADITION

The Foundation for the Preservation of the Mahayana Tradition (FPMT) is an international organization of Buddhist meditation study and retreat centers, both urban and rural, monasteries, publishing houses, healing centers and other related activities founded in 1975 by Lama Thubten Yeshe and Lama Thubten Zopa Rinpoche. At present, there are more than 160 FPMT activities in over thirty countries worldwide.

The FPMT has been established to facilitate the study and practice of Mahayana Buddhism in general and the Tibetan Gelug tradition, founded in the fifteenth century by the great scholar, yogi and saint, Lama Je Tsongkhapa, in particular.

Every quarter, the Foundation publishes a wonderful news journal, *Mandala*, from its International Office in the United States of America. To subscribe or view back issues, please go to the *Mandala* website, www.mandalamagazine.org, or contact:

FPMT
1632 SE 11th Avenue, Portland, OR 97214
Telephone (503) 808-1588; Fax (503) 808-1589
info@fpmt.org
www.fpmt.org

The FPMT website also offers teachings by His Holiness the Dalai Lama, Lama Yeshe, Lama Zopa Rinpoche and many other highly respected teachers in the tradition, details about the FPMT's educational programs, audio through FPMT radio, a link to the excellent FPMT Store, a complete listing of FPMT centers all over the world and in your area, and links to FPMT centers on the web, where you will find details of their programs, and to other interesting Buddhist and Tibetan home pages.

DISCOVERING BUDDHISM AT HOME
Awakening the limitless potential of your mind,
achieving all peace and happiness

Over 2500 years ago, Shakyamuni Buddha gained direct insight into the nature of reality, perfected the qualities of wisdom, compassion, and power, and revealed the path to his disciples. In the 11th Century, Atisha brought these teachings to Tibet in the form of the lam-rim—the stages on the path to enlightenment. The lam-rim tradition found its pinnacle in the teachings of the great Tibetan saint Je Tsongkhapa in the 14th Century, and these teachings continued to pass from teacher to student up to this present day.

When Lama Thubten Yeshe and Lama Zopa Rinpoche transmitted these teachings to their disciples, they imparted a deeply experiential tradition of study and practice, leading thousands of seekers to discover the truth of what the Buddha taught. This tradition is the core of *Discovering Buddhism*— a two-year, fourteen-module series that provides a solid foundation in the teachings and practice of Tibetan Mahayana Buddhism.

HOW IT WORKS: Each *Discovering Buddhism* module consists of teachings, meditations and practices, readings, assessment questions, and a short retreat. Students who complete all the components of each course receive a completion card. When all fourteen modules have been completed, students receive a certificate of completion, a symbol of commitment to spiritual awakening.

This program is offered in FPMT centers around the world, as a home study program and, beginning in 2009, as an interactive online program.

HOME STUDY PROGRAM: Each *Discovering Buddhism at Home* module contains audio recordings of teachings and meditations given by qualified Western teachers, and a text CD containing the course materials and transcripts of the audio teachings, and an online discussion board overseen by senior FPMT teachers. FAQ pages help the student navigate the program and provide the best of the discussion board's questions and answers. Upon completion of a module, students may have their assessment questions evaluated by senior FPMT teachers and receive personal feedback.

Discovering Buddhism at Home is available from the FPMT Foundation Store, www.fpmt.org/shop. For more information on *Discovering Buddhism* and the other educational programs and services of the FPMT, please visit us at www.fpmt.org/education.

Other teachings of Lama Yeshe and Lama Zopa Rinpoche currently available

Books published by Wisdom Publications
Wisdom Energy, by Lama Yeshe and Lama Zopa Rinpoche
Introduction to Tantra, by Lama Yeshe
Transforming Problems, by Lama Zopa Rinpoche
The Door to Satisfaction, by Lama Zopa Rinpoche
Becoming Vajrasattva: The Tantric Path of Purification, by Lama Yeshe
The Bliss of Inner Fire, by Lama Yeshe
Becoming the Compassion Buddha, by Lama Yeshe
Ultimate Healing, by Lama Zopa Rinpoche
Dear Lama Zopa, by Lama Zopa Rinpoche
How to Be Happy, by Lama Zopa Rinpoche
Wholesome Fear, by Lama Zopa Rinpoche with Kathleen McDonald

About Lama Yeshe:
Reincarnation: The Boy Lama, by Vicki Mackenzie

About Lama Zopa Rinpoche:
The Lawudo Lama, by Jamyang Wangmo

You can get more information about and order the above titles at www.wisdompubs.org or call toll free in the USA on 1-800-272-4050.

Transcripts, practices and other materials
See the LYWA and FPMT websites for transcripts of teachings by Lama Yeshe and Lama Zopa Rinpoche and other practices written or compiled by Lama Zopa Rinpoche.

DVDs of Lama Yeshe
We are in the process of converting our VHS videos of Lama Yeshe's teachings to DVD. *The Three Principal Aspects of the Path, Introduction to Tantra, Offering Tsok to Heruka Vajrasattva, Anxiety in the Nuclear Age, Bringing Dharma to the West* and *Lama Yeshe at Disneyland* are currently available. More coming all the time—see our website for details.

DVDs of Lama Zopa Rinpoche
There are many available: see the Store on the FPMT website
for more information.

WHAT TO DO WITH DHARMA TEACHINGS

The Buddhadharma is the true source of happiness for all sentient beings. Books like this show you how to put the teachings into practice and integrate them into your life, whereby you get the happiness you seek. Therefore, anything containing Dharma teachings, the names of your teachers or holy images is more precious than other material objects and should be treated with respect. To avoid creating the karma of not meeting the Dharma again in future lives, please do not put books (or other holy objects) on the floor or underneath other stuff, step over or sit upon them, or use them for mundane purposes such as propping up wobbly tables. They should be kept in a clean, high place, separate from worldly writings, and wrapped in cloth when being carried around. These are but a few considerations.

Should you need to get rid of Dharma materials, they should not be thrown in the rubbish but burned in a special way. Briefly: do not incinerate such materials with other trash, but alone, and as they burn, recite the mantra OM AH HUM. As the smoke rises, visualize that it pervades all of space, carrying the essence of the Dharma to all sentient beings in the six samsaric realms, purifying their minds, alleviating their suffering, and bringing them all happiness, up to and including enlightenment. Some people might find this practice a bit unusual, but it is given according to tradition. Thank you very much.

DEDICATION

Through the merit created by preparing, reading, thinking about and sharing this book with others, may all teachers of the Dharma live long and healthy lives, may the Dharma spread throughout the infinite reaches of space, and may all sentient beings quickly attain enlightenment.

In whichever realm, country, area or place this book may be, may there be no war, drought, famine, disease, injury, disharmony or unhappiness, may there be only great prosperity, may everything needed be easily obtained, and may all be guided by only perfectly qualified Dharma teachers, enjoy the happiness of Dharma, have love and compassion for all sentient beings, and only benefit and never harm each other.

LAMA THUBTEN ZOPA RINPOCHE was born in Thami, Nepal, in 1945. At the age of three he was recognized as the reincarnation of the Lawudo Lama, who had lived nearby at Lawudo, within sight of Rinpoche's Thami home. Rinpoche's own description of his early years may be found in his book, *The Door to Satisfaction*. At the age of ten, Rinpoche went to Tibet and studied and meditated at Domo Geshe Rinpoche's monastery near Pagri, until the Chinese occupation of Tibet in 1959 forced him to forsake Tibet for the safety of Bhutan. Rinpoche then went to the Tibetan refugee camp at Buxa Duar, West Bengal, India, where he met Lama Yeshe, who became his closest teacher. The Lamas went to Nepal in 1967, and over the next few years built Kopan and Lawudo Monasteries. In 1971 Lama Zopa Rinpoche gave the first of his famous annual lam-rim retreat courses, which continue at Kopan to this day. In 1974, with Lama Yeshe, Rinpoche began traveling the world to teach and establish centers of Dharma. When Lama Yeshe passed away in 1984, Rinpoche took over as spiritual head of the FPMT, which has continued to flourish under his peerless leadership. More details of Rinpoche's life and work may be found in *The Lawudo Lama* and on the LYWA and FPMT websites. In addition to many LYWA and FPMT books, Rinpoche's other published teachings include *Wisdom Energy* (with Lama Yeshe), *Transforming Problems, Ultimate Healing, Dear Lama Zopa, How to Be Happy, Wholesome Fear* and many transcripts and practice booklets.

AILSA CAMERON first met Buddhism at Tushita Retreat Centre in India in 1983 and has since been involved in various activities within the FPMT, primarily in relation to the archiving, transcribing and editing of the teachings of Lama Zopa Rinpoche and Lama Yeshe. With Ven. Robina Courtin, she edited *Transforming Problems* and *The Door to Satisfaction*, by Lama Zopa Rinpoche, and *The Bliss of Inner Fire*, by Lama Yeshe, for Wisdom Publications. She also edited Rinpoche's *Ultimate Healing* and *How to Be Happy* for Wisdom. After working originally in India and Nepal, she went to Hong Kong in 1989 to help organize the electronic version of the LAMA YESHE WISDOM ARCHIVE. Ordained as a nun by His Holiness the Dalai Lama in 1987, she has been a member of the Chenrezig Nuns' Community in Australia since 1990. She is currently a full time editor with the LAMA YESHE WISDOM ARCHIVE, for whom she has edited many teachings, including *Teachings from the Mani Retreat, Teachings from the Vajrasattva Retreat, How Things Exist, Heart of the Path* and *Teachings from the Medicine Buddha Retreat*.